Company's Coming®

Low-Fat Pasta

Jean Paré

www.**companys**coming.com
visit our web-site

Front Cover

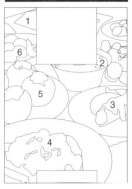

1. Radiatore With Roasted Pepper Salsa, page 66
2. Zuppa Fagioli, page 119
3. Chocolate Cheese Manicotti, page 45
4. Creamy Peppered Chicken Sauce, page 111
5. Stuffed Tomato Salad, page 98
6. Mushroom-Filled Tortellini With Herb Butter, page 148

Props Courtesy Of: Chintz & Company
Glasshouse

Back Cover

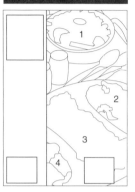

1. Roasted Chicken and Vegetables, page 30
2. Spaghetti and Marinated Tomatoes, page 79
3. Baked Mozza Rigatoni, page 73
4. Spinach Stuffed Cannelloni, page 139

Props Courtesy Of: Chintz & Company
Eaton's
Stokes
The Basket House

Low-Fat Pasta

Copyright © Company's Coming Publishing Limited
All rights reserved worldwide. No part of this book may be
reproduced in any form by any means without written
permission in advance from the publisher. Brief portions of this
book may be reproduced for review purposes, provided credit
is given to the source. Reviewers are invited to contact the
publisher for additional information.

First Printing February 2001

Canadian Cataloguing in Publication Data

Company's Coming low-fat pasta

Previously published as: Low-fat pasta. 1999.
Includes index.
ISBN 1-895455-84-7

    1. Cookery (Pasta) 2. Low-fat diet—Recipes. I. Paré, Jean. Low-fat Pasta.
I Title. II. Title: Low-fat pasta.

TX809.M17P372 2001   641.8'22   C00-901036-X

Originally published in the Lifestyle Series ISBN 1-896891-44-6

Published simultaneously in Canada and the United States of America by
COMPANY'S COMING PUBLISHING LIMITED
2311 - 96 Street
Edmonton, Alberta, Canada T6N 1G3
Tel: (780) 450-6223   Fax: (780) 450-1857
www.companyscoming.com

Company's Coming is a registered trademark owned by
Company's Coming Publishing Limited
Printed in Canada

Cooking Tonight?
Drop by companyscoming.com

| Who We Are | Browse Cookbooks | Cooking Tonight? | Home |

everyday ingredients

feature recipes

feature recipes — Cooking tonight? Check out this month's **feature recipes**—absolutely FREE!

tips and tricks — Looking for some great kitchen helpers? **tips and tricks** is here to save the day!

table talk — In search of answers to cooking or household questions? Do you have answers you'd like to share? Join the fun with **table talk**, our on-line question and answer bulletin board. Our **table talk chat room** connects you with cooks from around the world. Great for swapping recipes too!

cooking links — Other interesting and informative web-sites are just a click away with **cooking links.**

experts on-line — Consult **experts on-line** for Jean Paré's time-saving tips and advice.

keyword search — Find cookbooks by title, description or food category using **keyword search**.

e-mail us — We want to hear from you—**e-mail us** lets you offer suggestions for upcoming titles, or share your favorite recipes.

Company's Coming
COOKBOOKS®

everyday recipes trusted by millions

Company's Coming Cookbooks

Original Series

- 150 Delicious Squares
- Appetizers
- Barbecues
- Breads
- Breakfasts & Brunches
- Cakes
- Casseroles
- Chicken, Etc.
- Cookies
- Cooking for Two
- Desserts
- Dinners of the World
- Fish & Seafood

- Holiday Entertaining
- Kids Cooking
- Light Casseroles
- Light Recipes
- Low-Fat Cooking **NEW**
- Low-Fat Pasta **NEW**
- Lunches
- Main Courses
- Make-Ahead Meals
- Meatless Cooking
- Microwave Cooking
- Muffins & More
- One-Dish Meals

- Pasta
- Pies
- Pizza!
- Preserves
- Salads
- Slow Cooker Recipes
- Soups & Sandwiches
- Starters
- Stir-Fry
- The Potato Book **NEW**
- Vegetables

Greatest Hits Series

- Biscuits, Muffins & Loaves
- Dips, Spreads & Dressings
- Sandwiches & Wraps
- Soups & Salads

Lifestyle Series

- Grilling
- Low-Fat Cooking
- Low-Fat Pasta

Special Occasion Series

- Chocolate Everything **NEW**
- Easy Entertaining

Other

- Beef Today!

Table of Contents

The Company's Coming Story

Jean Paré grew up understanding that the combination of family, friends and home cooking is the essence of a good life. From her mother she learned to appreciate good cooking, while her father praised even her earliest attempts. When she left home she took with her many acquired family recipes, a love of cooking and an intriguing desire to read recipe books like novels!

"never share a recipe you wouldn't use yourself"

In 1963, when her four children had all reached school age, Jean volunteered to cater the 50th anniversary of the Vermilion School of Agriculture, now Lakeland College. Working out of her home, Jean prepared a dinner for over 1000 people which launched a flourishing catering operation that continued for over eighteen years. During that time she was provided with countless opportunities to test new ideas with immediate feedback—resulting in empty plates and contented customers! Whether preparing cocktail sandwiches for a house party or serving a hot meal for 1500 people, Jean Paré earned a reputation for good food, courteous service and reasonable prices.

"Why don't you write a cookbook?" Time and again, as requests for her recipes mounted, Jean was asked that question. Jean's response was to team up with her son, Grant Lovig, in the fall of 1980 to form Company's Coming Publishing Limited. April 14, 1981, marked the debut of "150 DELICIOUS SQUARES", the first Company's Coming cookbook in what soon would become Canada's most popular cookbook series.

Jean Paré's operation has grown steadily from the early days of working out of a spare bedroom in her home. Full-time staff includes marketing personnel located in major cities across Canada. Home Office is based in Edmonton, Alberta in a modern building constructed specially for the company.

Today the company distributes throughout Canada and the United States in addition to numerous overseas markets, all under the guidance of Jean's daughter, Gail Lovig. Best-sellers many times over, Company's Coming cookbooks are published in English and French, plus a Spanish-language edition is available in Mexico. Familiar and trusted in home kitchens the world over, Company's Coming cookbooks are offered in a variety of formats, including the original softcover series.

Jean Paré's approach to cooking has always called for quick and easy recipes using everyday ingredients. Even when traveling, she is constantly on the lookout for new ideas to share with her readers. At home, she can usually be found researching and  writing recipes, or working in the company's test kitchen. Jean continues to gain new supporters by adhering to what she calls "the golden rule of cooking": never share a recipe you wouldn't use yourself. It's an approach that works—*millions of times over!*

Foreword

Pasta is often thought of as fattening, but that isn't quite accurate. In fact, pasta is naturally high in complex carbohydrates, rich in protein, and low in sodium and fat. It offers an economical source of balanced nutrition, is fast and easy to prepare, and complements a host of other ingredients.

Pasta itself is not high in fat, but be aware of what else goes onto or into your dish. High fat culprits are often those creamy toppings and rich sauces that have been liberally served over pasta. *Low-Fat Pasta* focuses attention on keeping sauces low in fat, so if you are someone who loves to add lots of sauce to your pasta, this is your chance to do so guilt-free. By using less oil in tomato-based sauces and by substituting skim evaporated milk in rich cream sauces, we were able to considerably reduce fat content.

In addition to this great selection of recipes, *Low-Fat Pasta* offers an overview of the wide variety of pasta available, answers many frequently asked questions on proper cooking and storage of pasta, and reveals hidden secrets of pasta etiquette! Take a moment to enjoy reading these and other helpful cooking tips found throughout this book.

Each recipe includes a nutrition analysis which identifies calories, total fat, protein, sodium, carbohydrate and fiber content. To help you recognize high-risk fats, the total fat information has been broken down further into saturated fat and cholesterol. These analyses have been done using the ingredients listed in each recipe, with the exception of those identified as "optional" or "garnish". We have also used the first ingredient listed whenever a second alternative is

offered (such as "butter or hard margarine"). If a range of servings is offered in a recipe, we analyzed the first serving amount, which is the larger serving size.

Treat your family to new and exciting *Low-Fat Pasta* appetizers, soups, salads, main courses, fresh homemade pasta and much more! There are all kinds of terrific pasta dishes to explore, so dive into *Low-Fat Pasta* and get started. These inspirational recipes will bring brilliant colors and irresistible flavors to your dining experience.

Jean Paré

Each recipe has been analyzed using the most up-to-date version of the Canadian Nutrient File from Health Canada, which is based upon the United States Department of Agriculture (USDA) Nutrient Data Base.

Margaret Ng, B.Sc. (Hon), M.A.
Registered Dietitian

facts about fat

Calories are measurements of energy, and you need and get this energy on a daily basis from the nutrients in the foods you eat.

Fat, carbohydrate and protein are all energy nutrients, but fat offers a more concentrated source of energy (calories):

1 gram of fat = 9 calories

1 gram of protein = 4 calories

1 gram of carbohydrate = 4 calories

As you can see, fat contains over twice the amount of calories as carbohydrates or protein. How many calories your body requires is determined by a number of factors, including your size, weight and lifestyle. To find out how many calories are recommended for your daily intake, you should consult a dietician.

To maintain a healthy lifestyle it's recommended that no more than 30% of your daily energy intake come from fat, and no more than 10% of that should be saturated fat. This refers to total daily food intake and not just individual foods. So, it's okay to indulge in foods higher in fat, as long as you also eat foods lower in fat, for an average of 30% per day. Here's a quick way to calculate the percentage of fat found in a recipe or ingredient:

Fat (grams) x 9 (calories/gram)
= fat calories

(Fat calories ÷ total calories) x 100
= % calories from fat

¼ cup (60 mL) grated Cheddar cheese contains 113 calories and 9.3 grams of fat. Using this calculation, we can determine that:

9.3 grams x 9 calories/gram
= 83.7 fat calories

(83.7 fat calories ÷ 113 total calories) x 100 = 74% calories from fat

Many people find it easier to calculate their daily fat allowance in grams instead of percentages. To do this you need to know what your daily calorie intake should be. For example, if your energy intake is 1500 calories per day and your goal is 30% calories from fat:

1500 total calories x 0.30 from fat
= 500 fat calories

500 fat calories ÷ 9 calories/gram
= 56 grams of fat per day

types of fat

Different types of fat find their way into your diet and each has a different effect on the body. Saturated fats are a kind of fat that our bodies don't easily break down, and it's this kind of fat that can be associated with certain forms of cancer, increased cholesterol levels and risk of heart disease. Unsaturated fats (monounsaturated and polyunsaturated) are less harmful than saturated fats and may even help lower total cholesterol and triglyceride levels. Unfortunately, too much of this fat can also contribute to obesity, gallstones and certain cancers. Hydrogenated fats start out as a liquid but become solid when hydrogen bonds are added. This type of fat has the same health effects as saturated fats. Cholesterol is produced naturally by your body and can be found in foods of animal origin (meats, fish, poultry, eggs and dairy products). When an excess amount of cholesterol is present in the blood, it tends to deposit in the arteries.

alternatives to high-fat products

Milk: Recipes in *Low-Fat Pasta* that include milk have been tested using skim milk. Skim evaporated milk was used in place of heavy cream or whipping cream.

Cheese: Cheese is often a big culprit in adding fat to your diet, which is why *Low-Fat Pasta* uses low-fat or part-skim cheeses. We also reduced the amount of cheese per serving without sacrificing flavor, effectively lowering the fat content of a recipe.

Cooking with oils/fats: In this book, recipes that used oil were tested with canola or olive oil, both of which are high in unsaturated fat and low in saturated fat. Keep in mind that all oils, whether saturated or unsaturated, contain the same amount of fat and calories—it's only the type of fat (see page 8) that is different.

Eggs: Wherever possible, we used a frozen egg substitute product for eggs. This newer product is essentially eggs without the saturated fat found in the yolk:

1 large egg = ¼ cup (50-60 mL) frozen egg substitute product

Salad dressings and mayonnaise: Wherever possible, the recipes in *Low-Fat Pasta* use low-fat dressings and mayonnaise.

Margarine: Tub margarines contain more water and less fat than hard margarine or butter, and it's for this reason that *Low-Fat Pasta* recipes use tub margarine whenever possible. Diet tub margarine, which contains even more water but retains a buttery flavor, was used when flavor is more critical.

pasta facts

selecting the right kind of pasta

Commercial brands of pasta can vary in quality. A good quality pasta is made out of semolina, a durum wheat more coarsely ground than normal wheat flours, often obtained by sifting out the finer flour. Other commercial brands are satisfactory but their cooking times and textures can vary slightly.

We tested the recipes in this book using a large variety of commercial brand names to ensure that all pasta would work for any one of these recipes.

Basic pasta dough is made of flour and water, and sometimes enriched with egg. Adding eggs to pasta increases fat content slightly but turns out a tender, flavorful product. *Low-Fat Pasta* has made use of yolk-free pasta, an egg pasta that is lower in fat.

Pasta dough can also be flavored and colored by adding spinach, herbs, beets, tomatoes, saffron and so on. Try making your own flavored fresh pasta with an assortment of herbs from the Pasta-Making section of this book.

Choose whole wheat pasta for a healthy, high fiber diet; it not only contains the B vitamins and iron, it also provides many trace vitamins and minerals.

the secrets of success to cooking pasta

Amount of pasta: In *Low-Fat Pasta* we allowed 2 to 3 oz. (57-85 g) uncooked pasta per serving. Actual amounts required will depend on the type and size of pasta chosen and what other side dishes will be served.

Size of saucepan: Use a large saucepan or Dutch oven that can hold at least 8 cups (2 L) of water and allows enough space for pasta to "swim" during cooking.

Amount of water: Pasta should be cooked in a large amount of water—at least 8 cups (2 L) for each 8 oz. (225 g) uncooked pasta. You may need more water for larger pasta such as rotini. Too little water can prevent the starch in pasta from releasing, leaving you with a sticky, starchy-tasting product. Add pasta after water comes to a full rolling boil— the rolling motion will help to cook it evenly with less sticking.

Salt or no salt? In these recipes we recommend 1 tsp. (5 mL) salt for every 4 cups (1 L) water. Salt helps prevent nutrients from leaching out of the pasta into the water. To prevent a film from forming around the edge of the Dutch oven, add salt after water has come to a rolling boil.

Is oil necessary? Oil is usually added to boiling water to prevent pasta from sticking, but because it adds unnecessary fat, we omitted it in these recipes. Stirring occasionally while cooking will keep pasta from sticking.

Stirring pasta: Once pasta has been added to boiling water, stir immediately with a long-handled spoon to prevent sticking in the saucepan, and continue to stir occasionally until pasta is cooked.

Checking for doneness: Because cooking times vary according to the size, thickness and ingredients of pasta, always cook for the minimum time stated in the recipe and then longer if required. To test for doneness, remove a piece of pasta with a fork or spoon and cool slightly before tasting. If it's tender, still holds its shape and is slightly firm or "al dente," then it is ready. The term al dente (pronounced al-DEN-tay) is an Italian phrase meaning "to the tooth." When bitten into, the pasta offers slight resistance and isn't soft or overcooked.

Draining pasta: Pour cooked pasta into a colander and drain well—water left on cooked pasta will dilute the sauce, making it thin and less flavorful.

Rinsing cooked pasta: Rinsing will remove excess salt from your pasta, but be aware it will also wash away some of the starch that helps sauces "cling." Definitely rinse pasta when using it in a salad, or if you don't plan to serve it right away; this will help prevent it from sticking together.

Storing pasta: Dry, uncooked pasta has an indefinite shelf life when kept tightly closed in the original package or in an airtight container in a cool, dry cupboard or shelf. To store cooked pasta, rinse thoroughly to prevent sticking before placing in a covered container in the refrigerator. If you're using cooked pasta the same day, pour enough cold water to cover it and place in the refrigerator until ready to use. Reheat in boiling water for 1 to 2 minutes until heated through. Freezing cooked pasta will change its texture and is therefore not recommended—although most pasta sauces freeze well. Fresh pasta can be stored loosely in a covered container for up to three days or frozen for up to one month. Kneaded pasta dough can be covered tightly with plastic wrap and frozen for up to six months. Before storing fresh pasta in the cupboard, make sure it's thoroughly dry to prevent mold. Use pasta racks or spread pasta out on clean towels to ensure fast, even drying. Drying time will depend on the thickness of the pasta, and air humidity. Store in an airtight container.

pasta etiquette

We often hear the question "What is the proper way to eat pasta?" The proper way is with a fork. Using a spoon is not recommended unless the sauce is very thin. Twirl a moderate amount of pasta around the tines of the fork and use the curve of the pasta bowl to help support the twirl. This is why pasta should be served in a wide, shallow bowl and not on a dinner plate. It's okay to allow a few strands of pasta to hang down off your fork; in fact, if pasta twirls too neatly and fully it is probably overcooked. Cutting pasta with a knife and fork is a major social blunder.

the pastabilities are endless!

There are so many shapes of pasta to choose from. This chart will help you select the correct pasta for your dish, and if you don't have the pasta called for in a recipe, simply pick a similar pasta from the same category.

varieties of pasta

String Pasta

Fine, delicate string pasta (such as capellini, vermicelli or rice vermicelli) are great served with light sauces and smaller cut ingredients. It's best to use a sauce that clings.

Capellini (ka-pe-LEE-nee) or angel-hair pasta: Round, extra thin noodle; also known as capelli d'angelo (ka-PELL-ee DAN-zheh-low) in Italian.

Fettuccine (feh-tuh-CHEE-nee): Flat, thin noodles ⅛-¼ inch (3-6 mm) wide.

Linguine (lin-GWEE-nee): Very narrow, flat, thick noodle approximately ⅛ inch (3 mm) wide.

Perciatelli (payr-chah-TEH-lee): Thicker, hollow version of spaghetti; also known as bucatini (book-kah-TEE-nee).

Rice vermicelli (also called rice-stick noodles): Round, very fine, transparent noodle made from rice flour.

Spaghetti (spuh-GEH-tee): Round, thin pasta. Comes from the Italian word for "strings."

Spaghettini: (spay-ghe-TEE-nee): Thinner variety of spaghetti.

Vermicelli (ver-mih-CHEH-lee): Very thin spaghetti, slightly thinner than spaghettini but not as thin as capellini.

Spiral Pasta

Great served with chunky sauces and in baked dishes.

Fusilli (fyoo-SEE-lee): Thin, corkscrew-shaped pasta, about 1½ inches (3.8 cm) long.

Gemelli (jay-MEH-lee): Short 1½ inch (3.8 cm) twists that resemble two strands of spaghetti twisted together.

Radiatore (rah-dyah-TOR-ay): Resembles little radiators with rippled edges.

Rotini (roh-TEE-nee): Corkscrew-shaped pasta about 1½ inches (3.8 cm) long, slightly thicker than fusilli.

Very Small (Tiny) Pasta

Especially good in soups or stews.

Acini di pepe (ah-CHEE-nee dee PAY-pay): Little peppercorn-shaped pasta.

Alphabets: Tiny letter-shaped pasta.

Anellini (ah-nehl-LEE-nee): Little ring-shaped pasta.

Conchigliette (kon-kee-YEH-tay): Smallest shell-shaped pasta available.

Farfallini (far-fah-LEE-nee): Smallest butterfly-shaped or bow tie pasta, with ruffled edge.

Orzo (OHR-zoh): Small rice-shaped pasta. Italian for "barley."

Quadrettini (kwah-dreh-TEE-nee): Small, flat square-shaped pasta.

Stelline (steh-LEE-nee): Small star-shaped pasta. Italian for "little stars."

Tripolini (tree-poh-LEE-nee): Very small bow tie pasta with rounded, rather than ruffled edge.

Tubetti (too-BEH-tee): Tiny narrow tube-shaped pasta. Italian for "little tubes."

Small Pasta

These are most commonly used in casseroles.

Cavatappi (kah-vah-TAH-pee): Short, corkscrew-shaped ribbed macaroni.

Conchiglie (kon-KEE-yay): Small shell-shaped pasta.

Ditali (dee-TAH-lee): Short straight tube-shaped pasta; a bit longer and wider than tubetti (see Very Small Pasta).

Elbow macaroni: Slightly curved tube-shaped smooth-surfaced pasta.

Medium Pasta

These shapes are all very good with tomato, meat or cream sauces and work well in casseroles.

Farfalle (far-FAH-lay): Butterfly-shaped or bow tie pasta, with ruffled edge.

Gnocchi (NYOH-kee): Small fresh pasta dumpling made from potato and flour. Eggs, cheese or spinach are popular additions; generally shaped into little balls and cooked in boiling water. A dry variation, made with durum semolina, is also available.

Grande conchiglie (kon-KEE-yay): Large shell-shaped pasta, either ridged or smooth-surfaced; cavity is excellent for trapping meat sauces or creamy sauces.

Orecchiette (oh-rayk-kee-EHT-tay): Small disk-shaped pasta; Italian for "little ears."

Penne (PEH-nay): Short, tube-shaped ribbed pasta about ¼ inch (6 mm) in diameter and 2 inches (5 cm) long, cut on the diagonal.

Rotelle (roh-TEL-lay): Wagon wheel-shaped pasta.

Ziti (ZEE-tee): Tube-shaped, smooth-surfaced macaroni, about ½ inch (12 mm) in diameter and 1½ inches (3.8 cm) long; similar to rigatoni (see Large Pasta).

Large Pasta

These pastas swell up quite large so be prepared; they can look impressive served in a large pasta bowl with a creamy or chunky, thick sauce that clings well; or bake with sauce for a casserole-type look.

Farfallone (far-fah-LOH-nee): Largest of the butterfly-shaped or bow tie pasta.

Lasagne (lah-ZAHN-yuh): Wide (about 2 inches, 5 cm), flat noodle, sometimes with ruffled edges.

Rigatoni (rig-ah-TOH-nee): Tube-shaped macaroni, about ½ inch (12 mm) in diameter and 2 inches (5 cm) long.

Stuffed Pasta

Delicious served with a variety of tomato or cream sauces.

Agnolotti (ah-nyoh-LAH-tee): Squares of pasta filled with meat or vegetables. Similar to ravioli, but slightly larger.

Cannelloni (kan-eh-LOH-nee): Large tube-shaped pasta (or square pasta that has been rolled into tube) that is boiled and then stuffed with a meat, cheese or vegetable filling.

Cappelletti (kah-peh-LEH-tee): Small dumplings made of 2 inch (5 cm) squares, stuffed and formed into a hat-like shape. Usually stuffed with ground beef, cheese or vegetables. The name is taken from the plural of the Italian word cappelletto, which means "little hat."

Conchiglioni (kon-KEE-yay-ON-ee): Jumbo shell-shaped pasta usually stuffed with cheese, meat or vegetable fillings.

Manicotti (man-eh-KAH-tee): Large tube-shaped ribbed pasta cut on the diagonal.

Pansotti (pan-SOH-tee): A stuffed triangular-shaped dumpling. Usually stuffed with cheese and spinach, swiss chard or borage (a European herb; used like spinach). Italian for "pot bellied."

Ravioli (rav-ee-OH-lee): A square-shaped (or sometimes round-shaped) pasta dumpling. Usually stuffed with meat, cheese or vegetable fillings.

Tortellini (tor-teh-LEE-nee): Small, ring-shaped pasta dumplings. Usually filled with meat or cheese.

Tortelloni (tor-teh-LOH-nee): Larger version of tortellini.

Specialty Pasta

Entertain any time of year with creative and fun seasonal-shaped pastas. Try little Christmas trees and angels at Christmastime, hearts on Valentine's Day, leaves and pumpkins at Thanksgiving … and more! This little extra touch will definitely add more flair to your festivities.

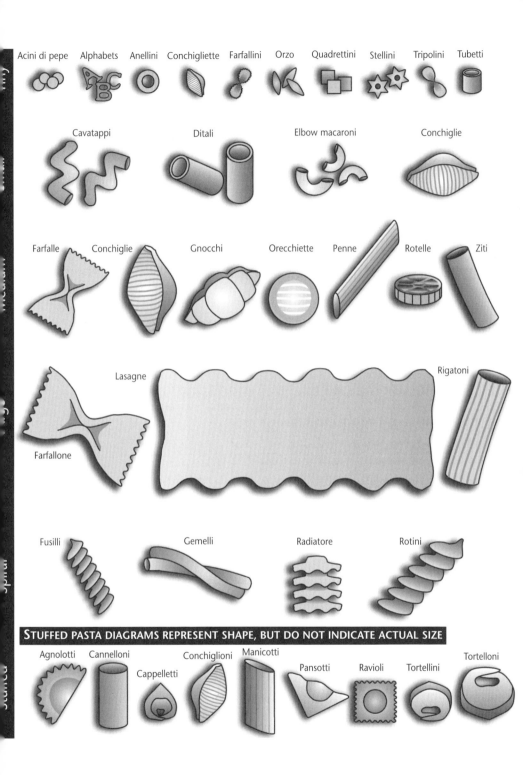

Acini di pepe Alphabets Anellini Conchigliette Farfallini Orzo Quadrettini Stellini Tripolini Tubetti

Cavatappi Ditali Elbow macaroni Conchiglie

Farfalle Conchiglie Gnocchi Orecchiette Penne Rotelle Ziti

Lasagne Rigatoni

Farfallone

Fusilli Gemelli Radiatore Rotini

STUFFED PASTA DIAGRAMS REPRESENT SHAPE, BUT DO NOT INDICATE ACTUAL SIZE

Agnolotti Cannelloni Conchiglioni Manicotti Pansotti Ravioli Tortellini Tortelloni
Cappelletti

13

Creamy Lox Shells

Lox is a type of smoked salmon that has been cured in brine and then cold-smoked. Slightly saltier than some other smoked salmons but can be used interchangeably.

Large (not jumbo) shell pasta (2½ oz., 70 g)	¾ cup	175 mL
Boiling water	4 cups	1 L
Salt	1 tsp.	5 mL
Light spreadable cream cheese	8 oz.	250 g
Low-fat salad dressing (or mayonnaise)	1 tbsp.	15 mL
Lemon juice	½ tsp.	2 mL
Freshly ground pepper, sprinkle		
Finely chopped lox (or smoked salmon)	⅓ cup	75 mL
Finely chopped fresh dill (or ½ tsp., 2 mL, dried)	2 tsp.	10 mL
Granulated sugar	⅛ tsp.	0.5 mL
Finely chopped ripe pitted olives (or pimiento), for garnish		

Cook pasta in boiling water and salt in large saucepan for 8 to 10 minutes, stirring occasionally, until tender but firm. Drain. Rinse with cold water until cool. Drain. Let stand on paper towel until dry.

Beat cream cheese, salad dressing and lemon juice together in small bowl until smooth. Add pepper, lox, dill and sugar. Mix well.

Spoon about 1 tsp. (5 mL) filling into each shell. Garnish with olives. Cover and refrigerate until cold. Makes about 60 shells.

1 filled shell: 15 Calories; 0.8 g Total Fat (0.4 g Sat., 2.4 mg Cholesterol); 72 mg Sodium; 1 g Protein; 1 g Carbohydrate; trace Dietary Fiber

Pictured on page 17.

Paré Pointer
That stamp is wet. Must be postage due.

Appetizer Cones

A creamy, yellow center. Preparation time is 20 minutes.

Very small pasta (such as bow tie, alphabet or orzo)	2/3 cup	150 mL
Boiling water	4 cups	1 L
Salt	1 tsp.	5 mL
Green onion, finely sliced	1	1
Very finely chopped dill pickles, blotted dry	1/2 cup	125 mL
Finely chopped celery	2 tbsp.	30 mL
Non-fat spreadable cream cheese	1/3 cup	75 mL
Skim milk	1 tbsp.	15 mL
Prepared mustard	1 tsp.	5 mL
Salt	1 tsp.	5 mL
Granulated sugar	1 tsp.	5 mL
Celery seed	1/4 tsp.	1 mL
Grated light Swiss cheese	1/2 cup	125 mL
Round non-fat ham slices (twelve 4 inch, 10 cm, round slices), cut in half	2 × 4 1/2 oz.	2 × 127 mL

Cook pasta in boiling water and first amount of salt in medium saucepan for 5 to 6 minutes, stirring occasionally, until tender but firm. Drain. Rinse with cold water. Drain.

Place pasta in medium bowl. Add next 3 ingredients.

Combine next 6 ingredients in small bowl. Mix until smooth. Add to pasta mixture. Add Swiss cheese. Mix well.

Shape 1 ham slice into cone shape. Hold in place with wooden pick. Place about 1 tbsp. (15 mL) pasta mixture inside each cone. Repeat with remaining ham slices and filling. Makes 24 appetizers.

1 appetizer: 47 Calories; 0.6 g Total Fat (0.3 g Sat., 1.5 mg Cholesterol); 306 mg Sodium; 3 g Protein; 7 g Carbohydrate; trace Dietary Fiber

Pictured on page 17.

Steak 'N' Penne

A hearty meal. Great served with a salad and bun.
Only ten minutes preparation time.

Lean boneless beef steak (such as top round), cut into ³/₄ inch (2 cm) cubes	1 lb.	454 g
Cooking oil	1 tsp.	5 mL
Chopped onion	1¹/₂ cups	375 mL
Garlic clove, minced (optional)	1	1
Condensed beef consommé	10 oz.	284 mL
Bay leaf	1	1
Pepper	¹/₄ tsp.	1 mL
Dried thyme	¹/₄ tsp.	1 mL
Parsley flakes	1 tbsp.	15 mL
Diced carrot	1¹/₂ cups	375 mL
Tomato (or vegetable) juice	2 cups	500 mL
Uncooked penne (medium tube pasta), 8 oz. (225 g)	2²/₃ cups	650 mL
Medium tomatoes, diced	2	2

Sauté beef cubes in oil in large non-stick skillet until browned. Add onion and garlic. Sauté until onion is soft.

Add next 6 ingredients. Stir. Bring to a boil. Cover. Simmer for 30 minutes. Discard bay leaf.

Stir in tomato juice. Bring to a boil. Add pasta. Cover. Simmer for 10 minutes. Remove cover. Cook until liquid is slightly evaporated and pasta is tender. Add tomato. Stir until warm. Serves 6.

1 serving: 287 Calories; 3.4 g Total Fat (0.8 g Sat., 27.7 mg Cholesterol); 606 mg Sodium; 23 g Protein; 41 g Carbohydrate; 3 g Dietary Fiber

Props Courtesy Of: Chintz & Company
The Basket House

Beef Dishes

Skillet Stroganoff

Very easy. Only 15 minutes preparation time.

Extra lean ground beef	¾ lb.	340 g
Finely chopped onion	½ cup	125 mL
Finely chopped celery	½ cup	125 mL
All-purpose flour	3 tbsp.	50 mL
Beef bouillon powder	2 tsp.	10 mL
Salt	½ tsp.	2 mL
Freshly ground pepper, sprinkle		
Water	2 cups	500 mL
Canned sliced mushrooms, with liquid	10 oz.	284 mL
Worcestershire sauce	1 tsp.	5 mL
Uncooked large yolk-free broad noodles (6 oz., 170 g)	3 cups	750 mL

Scramble-fry ground beef, onion and celery in large non-stick skillet or wok for 4 to 5 minutes until beef is no longer pink. Drain.

Sprinkle flour over beef mixture. Stir well. Stir in next 6 ingredients. Bring to a boil.

Add pasta. Cover. Simmer for 12 to 13 minutes, stirring occasionally, until pasta is tender but firm. Serves 4.

1 serving: 331 Calories; 8.1 g Total Fat (3 g Sat., 44 mg Cholesterol); 857 mg Sodium; 23 g Protein; 41 g Carbohydrate; 3 g Dietary Fiber

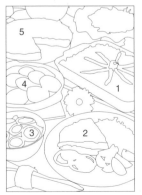

1. Chicken And Asparagus Pasta, page 43
2. Ground Beef And Spaghetti Pie, page 22
3. Warm Pepper And Lentil Medley, page 61
4. Ham And Noodle Bake, page 88
5. Garlic-Crusted Pasta Pie, page 20

Props Courtesy Of: Chintz & Company
                     Creations By Design
                     Eaton's

Garlic-Crusted Pasta Pie

You must be a garlic lover for this one! Firm enough to eat in your hands.

All-purpose flour	2 cups	500 mL
Instant dry yeast	1½ tsp.	7 mL
Granulated sugar	1 tsp.	5 mL
Garlic salt	½ tsp.	2 mL
Water	¾ cup	175 mL
Garlic cloves, minced	2	2
Olive oil	1 tsp.	5 mL
Cornmeal	1 tbsp.	15 mL
Garlic powder	⅛ tsp.	0.5 mL
Grated part-skim mozzarella cheese	½ cup	125 mL
Spaghetti (string pasta), broken into thirds	8 oz.	225 g
Boiling water	2 qts.	2 L
Salt	2 tsp.	10 mL
Lean ground beef	½ lb.	225 g
Chopped fresh mushrooms	½ cup	125 mL
Chopped green pepper	¼ cup	60 mL
Finely chopped onion	¼ cup	60 mL
Chopped ripe tomato	1 cup	250 mL
Tomato sauce	7.5 oz.	213 mL
Dried whole oregano	¾ tsp.	4 mL
Dried sweet basil	¾ tsp.	4 mL
Salt	½ tsp.	2 mL
Frozen egg product, thawed	3 tbsp.	50 mL
Grated part-skim mozzarella cheese	½ cup	125 mL
Grated light Parmesan cheese product	2 tbsp.	30 mL

Combine first 4 ingredients in medium bowl.

Heat water, garlic and oil in small saucepan or in microwave oven until very warm. Pour into dry ingredients. Stir together well until dough forms soft ball. Knead on lightly floured surface until smooth. Cover. Let rest in warm place for 15 minutes. Roll out on lightly floured surface to 12 inch (30 cm) circle. Grease deep 12 inch (30 cm) pizza pan.

Combine cornmeal and garlic powder in small bowl. Sprinkle in bottom of pizza pan. Fit crust into pan and form slightly raised edge. Sprinkle with first amount of mozzarella cheese.

(continued on next page)

Cook spaghetti in boiling water and first amount of salt in large saucepan or Dutch oven for 8 to 10 minutes, stirring occasionally, until tender but firm. Drain well. Place in even layer over cheese.

Scramble-fry ground beef, mushrooms, green pepper and onion in medium non-stick skillet until beef is browned. Drain. Stir in tomato and tomato sauce. Sauté for 2 to 3 minutes until tomato is soft. Add next 3 ingredients. Bring mixture to a boil. Remove from heat. Let cool slightly.

Stir in egg product. Pour mixture evenly over spaghetti and spread to pack down slightly into spaces. Sprinkle with second amount of mozzarella cheese and Parmesan cheese. Bake on center rack in 425°F (220°C) oven for 20 minutes until crust is browned and cheese is golden. Cuts into 8 wedges.

1 wedge: 346 Calories; 6.6 g Total Fat (2.8 g Sat., 24 mg Cholesterol); 547 mg Sodium; 18 g Protein; 53 g Carbohydrate; 3 g Dietary Fiber

Pictured on page 18.

 When sautéing vegetables or garlic in a smaller amount of oil, use a non-stick skillet; or, add a little extra liquid such as the juice from canned tomatoes or wine or broth to prevent burning.

Paré Pointer
When she phoned to say she couldn't meet him for lunch after all, he felt it was a big wait off his mind.

Ground Beef And Spaghetti Pie

Many ingredients but worth every one.
Takes about 35 minutes preparation time to get to the oven stage.

Spaghetti (string pasta)	6 oz.	170 g
Boiling water	6 cups	1.5 L
Salt	1½ tsp.	7 mL
Lean ground beef	¾ lb.	340 g
Chopped onion	1 cup	250 mL
Large garlic clove, minced	1	1
All-purpose flour	1½ tbsp.	25 mL
Granulated sugar	½ tsp.	2 mL
Ground cloves, sprinkle (optional)		
Ground nutmeg, sprinkle (optional)		
Canned stewed tomatoes, processed	14 oz.	398 mL
Frozen mixed vegetables	1 cup	250 mL
Frozen egg product, thawed	8 oz.	227 mL
Fine dry bread crumbs	¼ cup	60 mL
Beef bouillon powder	1 tsp.	5 mL
Skim milk	2 cups	500 mL
All-purpose flour	2 tbsp.	30 mL
Low-fat salad dressing (or mayonnaise)	1 tbsp.	15 mL
Grated light Cheddar cheese	½ cup	125 mL
Grated part-skim mozzarella cheese	½ cup	125 mL

Paprika, sprinkle
Chopped fresh parsley, for garnish

Cook pasta in boiling water and salt in large saucepan for 8 minutes, stirring occasionally, until tender but firm. Drain. Rinse with warm water. Drain.

Scramble-fry ground beef, onion and garlic in large non-stick skillet until no longer pink. Drain. Sprinkle with first amount of flour. Mix well. Stir in sugar, cloves, nutmeg, tomato and vegetables. Bring to a boil. Simmer, uncovered, for 15 minutes.

Place ½ of egg product in medium bowl. Add ground beef mixture. Add bread crumbs and bouillon powder. Mix well. Pour into lightly greased 10 inch (25 cm) glass pie plate. Spread cooked pasta evenly over top.

Gradually whisk milk into second amount of flour in medium saucepan until smooth. Cook, whisking often, until boiling and thickened. Remove from heat. Stir in salad dressing, Cheddar cheese and mozzarella cheese until melted. Stir in remaining ½ of egg product. Pour mixture evenly over pasta.

Sprinkle with paprika and parsley. Bake, uncovered, in 350°F (175°C) oven for 50 minutes until center is set and top is golden. Let stand for 10 minutes before cutting. Cuts into 8 wedges.

1 wedge: 294 Calories; 7.8 g Total Fat (3.4 g Sat., 32.1 mg Cholesterol); 448 mg Sodium; 22 g Protein; 34 g Carbohydrate; 2 g Dietary Fiber

Pictured on page 18.

Beef Dishes

Oriental Beef And Vegetables

Stir-fry served over pasta instead of rice! Cook pasta while cooking the beef and vegetables. Good reheated the next day.

Beef flank steak, cut on the diagonal into paper-thin 3 inch (7.5 cm) strips	8 oz.	225 g
Low-sodium soy sauce	1 tbsp.	15 mL
Garlic cloves, minced	2	2
Minced gingerroot	1 tsp.	5 mL
Vegetable oil	2 tsp.	10 mL
Prepared, frozen Oriental-style vegetables (see Note)	1 lb.	454 g
Canned sliced water chestnuts, drained	8 oz.	227 mL
Water	½ cup	125 mL
Sherry (or alcohol-free sherry)	2 tbsp.	30 mL
Chili sauce	2 tbsp.	30 mL
Low-sodium soy sauce	2 tbsp.	30 mL
Cooking (or fancy) molasses	1 tbsp.	15 mL
Cornstarch	1 tbsp.	15 mL
Vermicelli (string pasta)	8 oz.	225 g
Boiling water	2 qts.	2 L
Salt	2 tsp.	10 mL
Thinly sliced green onion	¼ cup	60 mL

Combine steak strips and first amount of soy sauce, garlic and ginger in small bowl. Let stand at room temperature for 10 minutes.

Heat non-stick wok or skillet until quite hot. Pour in oil. Add beef strips and marinade. Stir-fry quickly for about 2 minutes until just browned. Add vegetables and water chestnuts. Toss together well. Cover wok. Cook for 2 minutes. Stir. Cover. Cook for 2 minutes.

Combine next 6 ingredients in small bowl. Stir gently into beef and vegetables until mixture is boiling and thickened.

Cook pasta in boiling water and salt in Dutch oven for 5 to 6 minutes, stirring occasionally, until tender but firm. Drain. Arrange on platter with stir-fry beef over top. Sprinkle with green onion. Serves 4.

1 serving: 447 Calories; 7.7 g Total Fat (2.2 g Sat., 22.9 mg Cholesterol); 645 mg Sodium; 24 g Protein; 68 g Carbohydrate; 5 g Dietary Fiber

Pictured on page 89.

Note: You may substitute about 6 cups (1.5 L) prepared and steamed fresh vegetables.

Pastitsio

Pronounced pah-STEET-see-oh. A lower fat version of a rich, classic Greek recipe.
This dish can be assembled ahead of time and refrigerated. Simply bake when ready.

MEAT SAUCE

Chopped onion	1½ cups	375 mL
Tub margarine	1 tsp.	5 mL
Garlic cloves, minced	2	2
Extra lean ground beef	½ lb.	225 g
Lean ground lamb	½ lb.	225 g
Tomato sauce	14 oz.	398 mL
Salt	¾ tsp.	4 mL
Dried whole oregano	¼ tsp.	1 mL
Ground cinnamon	⅛ tsp.	0.5 mL
Bay leaf	1	1
Chopped fresh parsley (or 1 tbsp., 15 mL, dried)	3 tbsp.	50 mL

CUSTARD SAUCE

Skim milk	1 cup	250 mL
Skim evaporated milk	13½ oz.	385 mL
All-purpose flour	3 tbsp.	50 mL
Salt	⅛ tsp.	0.5 mL
Coarsely ground pepper	⅛ tsp.	0.5 mL
Ground nutmeg	1/16 tsp.	0.5 mL
Frozen egg product, thawed	8 oz.	227 mL
Elbow macaroni (small pasta), 12 oz. (340 g)	3 cups	750 mL
Boiling water	3 qts.	3 L
Salt	1 tbsp.	15 mL
Grated light Parmesan cheese product	¼ cup	60 mL
Grated Romano cheese	2 tbsp.	30 mL

(continued on next page)

Meat Sauce: Sauté onion in margarine in large non-stick skillet for 4 to 5 minutes until onion is soft and starting to turn golden. Stir in garlic, ground beef and ground lamb. Sauté for 4 to 5 minutes until meat is browned.

Stir in next 5 ingredients. Bring to a boil. Reduce heat. Simmer, partially covered, for 30 minutes. Discard bay leaf. Stir in parsley.

Custard Sauce: Slowly whisk both milks into flour in medium saucepan until smooth. Cook, stirring constantly, until boiling and thickened. Stir in salt, pepper and nutmeg. Pour egg product into medium bowl. Slowly whisk sauce into egg product until smooth.

Cook pasta in boiling water and salt in Dutch oven for 8 minutes, stirring occasionally. Pasta should be slightly undercooked. Drain. Rinse with warm water. Drain.

Place ½ of pasta in greased 9 x 13 inch (22 x 33 cm) baking dish. Sprinkle ½ of Parmesan cheese and ½ of Romano cheese over top. Cover with layers of meat sauce, remaining pasta and custard sauce. Sprinkle with remaining ½ of cheeses. Bake, uncovered, in 350°F (175°C) oven for 40 minutes until top is browned and bubbly. Let stand for 10 to 15 minutes to set before cutting into squares. Serves 8.

1 serving: 389 Calories; 7.9 g Total Fat (3 g Sat., 43.1 mg Cholesterol); 871 mg Sodium; 30 g Protein; 49 g Carbohydrate; 2 g Dietary Fiber

Pictured on page 54.

 To keep fresh basil green, place stems in a glass of water and keep on the counter for up to five days. Basil will turn brown if stored in the refrigerator.

Paré Pointer
It doesn't cost much to feed a giraffe. A little goes a long way.

Pepper Steak And Penne

Add more hot pepper sauce if you like to spice this up even more.
Only 15 minutes preparation time.

Top sirloin steak, cut into thin strips	1 lb.	454 g
Garlic cloves, minced	2	2
Hoisin sauce	2 tbsp.	30 mL
Vegetable oil	1 tsp.	5 mL
Pepper	¼ tsp.	1 mL
Medium green, red, orange or yellow peppers, slivered	3	3
Green onions, sliced	3	3
Condensed beef consommé	10 oz.	284 mL
Thinly sliced green cabbage	4 cups	1 L
Low-sodium soy sauce	¼ cup	60 mL
Cornstarch	2 tbsp.	30 mL
Hot pepper sauce	¼ tsp.	1 mL
Penne (medium tube pasta), 12 oz. (340 g)	4 cups	1 L
Boiling water	4 qts.	4 L
Salt	4 tsp.	20 mL
Toasted sesame seeds	2 tsp.	10 mL

Stir-fry steak strips, garlic and hoisin sauce in oil in large non-stick skillet or wok for about 5 minutes until beef is browned. Do not drain. Sprinkle with pepper.

Add green pepper, green onion and beef consommé. Bring to a boil. Cover. Simmer for 3 minutes. Stir in cabbage.

Combine soy sauce, cornstarch and hot pepper sauce in small cup. Mix well. Add to cabbage mixture. Cook, stirring often, until liquid is clear and thickened.

Cook pasta in boiling water and salt in Dutch oven for 12 to 14 minutes, stirring occasionally, until tender but firm. Drain. Combine pasta with beef and vegetable mixture.

Sprinkle with sesame seeds. Serves 6.

1 serving: 386 Calories; 5.3 g Total Fat (1.3 g Sat., 35.9 mg Cholesterol); 997 mg Sodium; 28 g Protein; 56 g Carbohydrate; 3 g Dietary Fiber

Beef Dishes

Sauced Beef And Mushrooms On Rotini

Toss with sauce before serving for a most appealing look.

Lean tender beef (top sirloin or tenderloin), thinly sliced into strips	10 oz.	285 g
Cooking oil	1 tsp.	5 mL
Finely chopped onion	¼ cup	60 mL
Garlic cloves, minced	2	2
Large fresh portobello mushrooms	2	2
Pepper, sprinkle		
Beef bouillon powder	2 tsp.	10 mL
Skim milk	1 cup	250 mL
All-purpose flour	2 tbsp.	30 mL
Skim evaporated milk	½ cup	125 mL
Rotini (spiral pasta), 8 oz. (225 g)	3 cups	750 mL
Boiling water	2 qts.	2 L
Salt	2 tsp.	10 mL

Sauté beef strips in oil with onion and garlic in large non-stick skillet for about 3 minutes until onion is soft.

Prepare mushrooms by trimming stem and dark "gills" off with sharp knife. Rinse and blot dry. Dice mushrooms into about ½ inch (12 mm) pieces and add to beef. Sprinkle with pepper. Simmer, stirring frequently, for 2 to 3 minutes until liquid is released from mushrooms. Stir in bouillon powder. Simmer until almost all liquid is evaporated.

Whisk milk into flour in small bowl until smooth. Pour into mushroom mixture along with evaporated milk. Cook, stirring frequently, until boiling and thickened.

Cook pasta in boiling water and salt in large saucepan for 10 to 12 minutes, stirring occasionally, until tender but firm. Drain. Toss with beef mixture. Serves 4.

1 serving: 401 Calories; 5.5 g Total Fat (1.4 g Sat., 36.4 mg Cholesterol); 421 mg Sodium; 27 g Protein; 57 g Carbohydrate; 3 g Dietary Fiber

Mexican Pasta Casserole

The corn-flavored pasta gives this dish a Mexican kick.

Corn-flavored rotini (spiral pasta), 10 oz. (285 g)	4½ cups	1.1 L
Boiling water	3 qts.	3 L
Salt	1 tbsp.	15 mL
Lean ground beef	¾ lb.	340 g
Garlic cloves, minced	2	2
Medium onions, halved lengthwise and sliced	2	2
Chopped green or red pepper	1 cup	250 mL
Canned kernel corn, drained (or 1 cup, 250 mL, frozen, thawed)	12 oz.	341 mL
Canned diced green chilies, drained	4 oz.	114 mL
Canned crushed tomatoes	14 oz.	398 mL
Canned black beans, drained and rinsed	19 oz.	540 mL
Salt	½ tsp.	2 mL
Ground cumin	¼ tsp.	1 mL
Ground coriander	¼ tsp.	1 mL
Dried crushed chilies	⅛ tsp.	0.5 mL
Pepper	⅛ tsp.	0.5 mL
Grated light Monterey Jack cheese	1 cup	250 mL

Cook pasta in boiling water and first amount of salt in Dutch oven for 8 to 10 minutes, stirring occasionally, until tender but firm. Drain. Rinse with warm water. Drain. Return to Dutch oven.

Scramble-fry ground beef, garlic, onion and green pepper in large non-stick skillet. Drain. Add to pasta. Mix well.

Add next 9 ingredients. Mix well. Pour into greased 4 quart (4 L) casserole dish. Cover. Bake in 350°F (175°C) oven for 30 minutes. Remove cover.

Sprinkle cheese over top. Bake, uncovered, for 10 minutes until bubbling and cheese is melted. Serves 6.

1 serving: 471 Calories; 9.6 g Total Fat (4.2 g Sat., 41 mg Cholesterol); 672 mg Sodium; 29 g Protein; 69 g Carbohydrate; 6 g Dietary Fiber

Pictured on page 36.

Chicken And Vegetable Stir-Fry

Rice stick noodles are long, flat, clear noodles that come in a variety of sizes.

Boneless, skinless chicken breast halves (about 3), sliced paper-thin	3/4 lb.	340 g
Garlic clove, minced	1	1
Cooking oil	1 tsp.	5 mL
Thinly sliced carrot, cut on the diagonal	2/3 cup	150 mL
Medium onion, cut into wedges	1	1
Thinly sliced celery, cut on the diagonal	2/3 cup	150 mL
Green, red, orange or yellow pepper, cut bite size	1/2	1/2
Fresh bean sprouts (10 oz., 285 g)	4 cups	1 L
Water	1 1/2 cups	375 mL
Low-sodium soy sauce	3 tbsp.	50 mL
Liquid chicken bouillon	2 tsp.	10 mL
Oyster sauce	1 tsp.	5 mL
Cornstarch	2 tbsp.	30 mL
Brown sugar, just a pinch		
Pepper	1/16 tsp.	0.5 mL
Package rice stick noodles (available at larger grocery stores)	1/2 × 1 lb.	1/2 × 454 g
Boiling water	2 qts.	2 L
Salt	2 tsp.	10 mL

Sauté chicken and garlic in oil in large non-stick skillet or wok for 4 to 5 minutes until chicken is no longer pink. Remove to medium bowl with slotted spoon, leaving any liquid in skillet. Add 2 tsp. (10 mL) water to skillet if there is no liquid left.

Stir in carrot. Cover. Cook for 1 minute. Add onion, celery and green pepper. Stir-fry for 1 minute. Scatter bean sprouts over top. Cover. Cook for 1 to 2 minutes. Make a well in center of vegetable mixture.

Combine next 7 ingredients in separate medium bowl. Mix. Pour into well. Stir until thickened and clear in color. Add chicken. Stir well.

Cook noodles in boiling water and salt in large saucepan for 5 minutes, stirring occasionally. Remove from heat. Let stand for 1 minute. Drain. Rinse with warm water. Drain. Serve chicken mixture over noodles. Serves 4.

1 serving: 407 Calories; 3.2 g Total Fat (0.5 g Sat., 49.5 mg Cholesterol); 990 mg Sodium; 28 g Protein; 66 g Carbohydrate; 3 g Dietary Fiber

Roasted Chicken And Vegetables

Chicken and vegetables are served over penne pasta. Thickening the sauce is optional.

Boneless, skinless chicken breast halves (about 4), cut into ¼ inch (6 mm) slivers	1 lb.	454 g
Non-fat Italian dressing	½ cup	125 mL
Non-fat Italian dressing	½ cup	125 mL
Garlic clove, minced	1	1
Dried sweet basil	¼ tsp.	1 mL
Dried rosemary, crushed	⅛ tsp.	0.5 mL
Large onion, cut into wedges	1	1
Small green or red peppers, cut into ½ inch (12 mm) slivers	2	2
Medium zucchini, with peel, sliced ¼ inch (6 mm) thick	1	1
Medium plum tomatoes, cut into ½ inch (12 mm) slices	3	3
Olive oil	2 tsp.	10 mL
Cornstarch (optional)	2 tsp.	10 mL
White wine (or water), optional	1 tbsp.	15 mL
Penne (medium tube pasta), 8 oz. (225 g)	2⅔ cups	650 mL
Boiling water	3 qts.	3 L
Salt	1 tbsp.	15 mL
Freshly ground pepper, sprinkle		
Grated light Parmesan cheese product, sprinkle (optional)		

Combine chicken and first amount of dressing. Set aside.

Combine second amount of dressing, garlic, basil and rosemary in large bowl. Add onion, green pepper and zucchini. Stir until lightly coated with dressing. Add chicken mixture. Mix well. Spread evenly on baking sheet with sides greased with oil. Bake on top rack in 450°F (230°C) oven for 10 minutes. Add tomato. Bake for 5 to 10 minutes until chicken is no longer pink and vegetables are tender-crisp.

For a thicker sauce, combine cornstarch and wine in small saucepan. Add liquid from cooked chicken and vegetables. Heat, stirring constantly, until boiling and thickened. Add to chicken and vegetables. Stir.

Cook pasta in boiling water and salt in Dutch oven for 8 to 10 minutes, stirring occasionally, until tender but firm. Drain. Toss with chicken and vegetables.

Sprinkle with pepper and Parmesan cheese. Makes 6½ cups (1.6 L) to pour over pasta. Serves 4.

1 serving: 446 Calories; 5.2 g Total Fat (0.9 g Sat., 65.8 mg Cholesterol); 798 mg Sodium; 36 g Protein; 63 g Carbohydrate; 4 g Dietary Fiber

Pictured on page 72 and back cover.

Chick 'N' Chili Penne

Chili served over pasta. Very colorful.

Water	¼ cup	60 mL
Chicken bouillon powder	1 tsp.	5 mL
Chili powder	½ tsp.	2 mL
Ground cumin	¼ tsp.	1 mL
Cayenne pepper, sprinkle		
Boneless, skinless chicken breast halves (about 2), cut into ¾ inch (2 cm) cubes	¾ lb.	340 g
Diced onion	1½ cups	375 mL
Large carrot, grated	1	1
Diced green pepper	1½ cups	375 mL
Canned stewed tomatoes, with juice, chopped	14 oz.	398 mL
Canned kidney beans, with liquid	14 oz.	398 mL
Salt	½ tsp.	2 mL
Pepper, sprinkle		
Chili powder	½ tsp.	2 mL
Ground cumin	¼ tsp.	1 mL
Penne (medium tube pasta), 8 oz. (225 g)	2⅔ cups	650 mL
Boiling water	3 qts.	3 L
Salt	1 tbsp.	15 mL

Combine first 5 ingredients in large non-stick skillet. Bring to a boil.

Add chicken, onion and carrot. Cook, stirring often, until liquid is evaporated and chicken is no longer pink. Add green pepper. Cook for 2 minutes.

Add tomato and kidney beans. Add first amount of salt, pepper and second amounts of chili powder and cumin. Bring to a boil. Reduce heat. Simmer, uncovered, for 1 hour until thickened.

Cook pasta in boiling water and second amount of salt in Dutch oven for 10 minutes, stirring occasionally, until tender but firm. Drain. Serve chili over pasta. Serves 6.

1 serving: 312 Calories; 2 g Total Fat (0.4 g Sat., 32.9 mg Cholesterol); 816 mg Sodium; 23 g Protein; 51 g Carbohydrate; 8 g Dietary Fiber

Pictured on page 36.

Chicken Pasta Casserole

Good, basic casserole for a rainy day.

Lean ground chicken	1 lb.	454 g
Garlic clove, minced	1	1
Medium onion, chopped	1	1
Salt	½ tsp.	2 mL
Pepper, sprinkle		
Celery rib, chopped	1	1
Medium carrot, grated	1	1
All-purpose flour	2 tbsp.	30 mL
Frozen peas	1 cup	250 mL
Uncooked elbow macaroni or fusilli (spiral pasta), 4 oz. (113 g)	1 cup	250 mL
Water	1 cup	250 mL
Chicken bouillon powder	2 tsp.	10 mL
Skim evaporated milk	¾ cup	175 mL
Coarsely crushed flakes of corn cereal	¼ cup	60 mL
Grated low-fat Swiss cheese	¼ cup	60 mL

Scramble-fry chicken, garlic and onion in medium non-stick skillet for 5 minutes. Sprinkle with salt and pepper. Add celery, carrot and flour. Stir together. Cook for about 1 minute.

Place ½ of chicken mixture in bottom of greased 2 quart (2 L) casserole dish. Scatter with peas and macaroni. Heat water, bouillon powder and evaporated milk in small saucepan until almost boiling. Pour ½ over macaroni. Cover with remaining chicken mixture and then remaining sauce. Cover. Bake in 350°F (175°C) oven for 45 minutes until pasta is cooked and most liquid is absorbed.

Combine cereal and cheese in small bowl. Sprinkle over casserole. Bake, uncovered, in 350°F (175°C) oven for 10 to 15 minutes until topping is browned. Serves 4.

1 serving: 382 Calories; 5.4 g Total Fat (1.8 g Sat., 80.3 mg Cholesterol); 967 mg Sodium; 36 g Protein; 46 g Carbohydrate; 4 g Dietary Fiber

Sauced Chicken With Pasta Pancakes

Each pasta pancake is thin and large—the size of the bottom of a medium skillet.

PASTA PANCAKES

Angel hair (very thin string) pasta (capellini)	1 lb.	454 g
Boiling water	4 qts.	4 L
Salt	4 tsp.	20 mL

(continued on next page)

All-purpose flour	¼ cup	60 mL
Sliced green onion	¼ cup	60 mL
Frozen egg product, thawed	¾ cup	175 mL
Low-sodium soy sauce	1 tbsp.	15 mL
Cooking oil, divided	2 tsp.	10 mL
SAUCED CHICKEN		
Boneless, skinless chicken breast halves (about 4), cut into thin strips	1 lb.	454 g
Garlic clove, minced	1	1
Low-sodium soy sauce	1 tbsp.	15 mL
Sherry (or alcohol-free sherry)	2 tsp.	10 mL
Cooking oil	1 tsp.	5 mL
Sliced fresh mushrooms	2 cups	500 mL
Fresh bean sprouts (8 oz., 225 g)	3¼ cups	800 mL
Condensed chicken broth	10 oz.	284 mL
Low-sodium soy sauce	2 tbsp.	30 mL
Water	¾ cup	175 mL
Cornstarch	3 tbsp.	50 mL
Sliced green onion	¼ cup	60 mL

Pasta Pancakes: Cook pasta in boiling water and salt in Dutch oven for 5 to 6 minutes, stirring occasionally. Do not overcook. Drain. Return to Dutch oven.

Combine flour and first amount of green onion in small cup. Sprinkle over pasta. Toss well. Mix egg product and soy sauce. Pour over pasta mixture. Toss well.

Divide mixture into 6 portions. Place 1 portion in medium non-stick skillet in ¼ to ½ tsp. (1 to 2 mL) oil. Press down with lightly greased pancake lifter to pack well. Cover. Cook for about 3 minutes on each side until golden and firm. Repeat for remaining 5 portions. Place on ungreased baking sheet. Keep warm in 200°F (95°C) oven.

Sauced Chicken: Combine chicken, garlic, first amount of soy sauce, sherry and oil in medium bowl. Marinate at room temperature for 10 minutes. Heat large non-stick skillet or wok until hot. Add chicken and marinade. Stir-fry for 2 minutes until chicken is separated but not completely cooked. Stir in mushrooms and bean sprouts. Stir-fry for 3 minutes. Stir in chicken broth and second amount of soy sauce.

Combine water and cornstarch in small bowl. Add to chicken mixture. Stir until boiling and thickened.

Stir in green onion. Makes 5 cups (1.25 L) sauced chicken. Serve over pancakes. Serves 6.

1 serving: 483 Calories; 5.4 g Total Fat (0.8 g Sat., 44.4 mg Cholesterol); 853 mg Sodium; 36 g Protein; 71 g Carbohydrate; 3 g Dietary Fiber

Pictured on page 144.

Chicken And Orzo

Very easy. Only 20 minutes preparation time.

Boneless, skinless chicken breast halves (about 2), sliced paper-thin	½ lb.	225 g
Garlic cloves, minced	2	2
Olive oil	1 tsp.	5 mL
Condensed chicken broth	10 oz.	284 mL
Water	1 cup	250 mL
Low-sodium soy sauce	1 tbsp.	15 mL
Medium carrot, cut julienne	1	1
Uncooked orzo (very small pasta)	1 cup	250 mL
Small zucchini, cut julienne	1	1
Medium red pepper, quartered lengthwise and sliced crosswise	1	1

Stir-fry chicken and garlic in oil in large non-stick skillet or wok for 5 minutes until chicken is almost cooked.

Add next 5 ingredients. Cover. Simmer for 10 minutes.

Stir in zucchini and red pepper. Cover. Cook for 5 minutes until pasta is tender and liquid is absorbed. Serves 4.

1 serving: 351 Calories; 3.7 g Total Fat (0.7 g Sat., 33.4 mg Cholesterol); 749 mg Sodium; 26 g Protein; 52 g Carbohydrate; 3 g Dietary Fiber

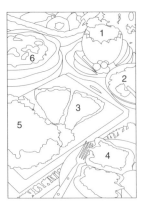

Props Courtesy Of: Le Gnome
The Basket House
The Bay

Brothed Chicken And Pea Pods With Penne

This is like a soup.

Chopped red or mild onion	¼ cup	60 mL
Garlic cloves, minced	2	2
Olive oil	1 tsp.	5 mL
Boneless, skinless chicken breast halves (about 4), cut bite size	1 lb.	454 g
White (or alcohol-free white) wine	2 tbsp.	30 mL
Condensed chicken broth	10 oz.	284 mL
Water	½ cup	125 mL
Fresh pea pods, trimmed (7 oz., 200 g)	3 cups	750 mL
Chopped fresh parsley	2 tbsp.	30 mL
Penne (medium tube pasta), 8 oz. (225 g)	2⅔ cups	650 mL
Boiling water	3 qts.	3 L
Salt	1 tbsp.	15 mL
Freshly ground pepper, sprinkle		

Sauté onion and garlic in oil in large saucepan, stirring constantly, for about 30 seconds. Turn heat to medium-high. Add chicken and wine. Cook, stirring frequently, for about 5 minutes until all liquid is evaporated and chicken is golden.

Stir in chicken broth, water and pea pods. Simmer, covered, for about 4 minutes until pea pods are bright green and tender-crisp. Stir in parsley. Keep warm.

Cook pasta in boiling water and salt in Dutch oven for 8 to 10 minutes, stirring occasionally, until tender but firm. Drain. Divide among 4 pasta bowls. Ladle chicken mixture over pasta. Sprinkle with pepper. Serve immediately. Serves 4.

1 serving: 405 Calories; 4.4 g Total Fat (0.9 g Sat., 69.2 mg Cholesterol); 556 mg Sodium; 39 g Protein; 48 g Carbohydrate; 3 g Dietary Fiber

1. Mexican Pasta Casserole, page 28
2. Stephe's Fiery Pasta, page 65
3. Chick 'N' Chili Penne, page 31
4. Mexican Chicken Rolls, page 150
5. Chicken Fajita Pasta, page 40

Props Courtesy Of: Stokes

Hungarian Chicken And Noodles

Try Hungarian paprika for a more pungent flavor.

Boneless, skinless chicken breast halves (about 4), sliced paper-thin	1 lb.	454 g
Canola (or vegetable) oil	1 tsp.	5 mL
Large red pepper, quartered lengthwise and sliced crosswise	1	1
Medium mild onion (Spanish or white), halved and thinly sliced	1	1
Hungarian (or regular) paprika	2 tbsp.	30 mL
Caraway seed (optional)	1 tsp.	5 mL
White (or alcohol-free white) wine	½ cup	125 mL
Skim evaporated milk	½ cup	125 mL
All-purpose flour	2 tbsp.	30 mL
Tomato paste	2 tbsp.	30 mL
Salt	1 tsp.	5 mL
Pepper	¼ tsp.	1 mL
Non-fat sour cream	1 cup	250 mL
Large yolk-free broad noodles (8 oz., 225 g)	4 cups	1 L
Boiling water	2 qts.	2 L
Salt	2 tsp.	10 mL

Stir-fry chicken in oil in large non-stick skillet for 4 minutes. Add red pepper and onion. Stir-fry for 5 minutes until chicken is no longer pink and pepper is tender-crisp.

Stir in paprika, caraway seed and wine.

Combine evaporated milk and flour in small cup. Mix until smooth. Stir into chicken mixture. Add tomato paste, first amount of salt and pepper. Stir until chicken mixture is boiling and thickened. Remove from heat. Stir in sour cream. Cover to keep warm. Makes 4 cups (1 L).

Cook pasta in boiling water and second amount of salt in Dutch oven for about 9 minutes, stirring occasionally, until tender but firm. Drain. Place on serving platter. Pour chicken mixture over. Serves 4.

1 serving: 455 Calories; 4.2 g Total Fat (0.7 g Sat., 67.1 mg Cholesterol); 830 mg Sodium; 40 g Protein; 59 g Carbohydrate; 3 g Dietary Fiber

Chicken Dishes

Easy Teriyaki Chicken Pasta

Fresh ginger gives this dish real zing!

Ingredient	Imperial	Metric
Low-sodium soy sauce	1/3 cup	75 mL
Brown sugar, packed	3 tbsp.	50 mL
Grated gingerroot	1/2 tsp.	2 mL
Garlic cloves, minced	2	2
Boneless, skinless chicken breast halves (about 3), thinly sliced	3/4 lb.	340 g
Cooking oil	1 tsp.	5 mL
Medium red pepper, diced	1	1
Medium yellow pepper, diced	1	1
Canned sliced water chestnuts, drained	8 oz.	227 mL
Cornstarch	2 tbsp.	30 mL
Canned pineapple tidbits, drained and juice reserved	14 oz.	398 mL
Fresh bean sprouts (6 oz., 170 g)	2 1/2 cups	625 mL
Green onions, thinly sliced	3	3
Angel hair (very thin string) pasta (capellini)	10 oz.	285 g
Boiling water	3 qts.	3 L
Salt	1 tbsp.	15 mL

Combine soy sauce, brown sugar, ginger and garlic in small cup. Stir until sugar is dissolved. Place chicken slices in medium bowl. Pour 3 tbsp. (50 mL) soy sauce mixture over chicken. Stir to coat chicken. Let stand for 10 minutes.

Sauté chicken in oil in large non-stick skillet for 2 minutes. Stir in peppers, water chestnuts and pineapple. Cover. Cook for about 3 minutes until peppers are tender-crisp. Make a well in center.

Combine cornstarch, reserved pineapple juice and remaining soy sauce mixture in small bowl. Mix well. Pour into center of chicken mixture. Sprinkle bean sprouts and green onion over top. Do not stir. Cover. Cook for about 2 minutes until boiling and thickened. Mix well.

Cook pasta in boiling water and salt in Dutch oven for 5 to 6 minutes, stirring occasionally, until tender but firm. Drain. Rinse with hot water. Drain. Place pasta on serving platter. Serve chicken mixture over pasta. Serves 6.

1 serving: 369 Calories; 2.4 g Total Fat (0.4 g Sat., 32.9 mg Cholesterol); 626 mg Sodium; 22 g Protein; 65 g Carbohydrate; 3 g Dietary Fiber

Pictured on page 71.

Chicken Fajita Pasta

*Using a cast-iron skillet sears the chicken wonderfully
and gives this dish its delicious flavor.*

Beer (or water)	1/2 cup	125 mL
Juice and grated peel of 1 small lime		
Lemon juice	1 tbsp.	15 mL
Garlic cloves, minced	2	2
Dried whole oregano, crushed	1 tsp.	5 mL
Onion powder	1/2 tsp.	2 mL
Ground cumin	1/4 tsp.	2 mL
Dried crushed chilies	1/2 tsp.	2 mL
Coarsely ground pepper	1/4 tsp.	2 mL
Boneless, skinless chicken breast halves (about 4)	1 lb.	454 g
Salt	1/2 tsp.	2 mL
Granulated sugar, just a pinch		
Cooking oil	1 tsp.	5 mL
Cooking oil	1 tsp.	5 mL
Medium red onion, cut in half lengthwise and thinly sliced	1	1
Green, red, orange or yellow peppers, sliced into thin slivers	2	2
Medium tomatoes, seeded and diced	2	2
Angel hair (very thin string) pasta (capellini)	10 oz.	285 g
Boiling water	3 qts.	3 L
Salt	1 tbsp.	15 mL

Combine first 9 ingredients in small bowl. Pour 1/2 of beer mixture into 10 inch (25 cm) glass pie plate for marinating. Add chicken. Turn to coat. Marinate at room temperature for 30 minutes. Sprinkle first amount of salt and sugar over remaining 1/2 of beer mixture in bowl. Stir to dissolve.

Heat large cast-iron skillet over medium until hot. Add first amount of oil. Place chicken in single layer in skillet. Spoon 2 tbsp. (30 mL) marinade from pie plate over chicken, discarding remaining marinade. Cover. Cook for 5 minutes. Turn chicken over. Cover. Cook for 5 minutes. Turn chicken over. Cook for 2 to 3 minutes until well browned and no longer pink. Cut chicken crosswise into thin slices. Place chicken slices and any liquid on plate. Cover to keep warm.

Add second amount of oil to hot skillet. Add onion and green pepper. Stir-fry for 1 minute. Pour in remaining beer mixture. Stir-fry for 1 minute, while scraping up any bits from skillet. Add chicken and liquid. Add tomato. Stir until tomato is hot. Place in large serving bowl.

(continued on next page)

Chicken Dishes

Cook pasta in boiling water and second amount of salt in Dutch oven for about 5 minutes, stirring occasionally, until tender but firm. Drain. Rinse with hot water. Drain. Pour over vegetable mixture. Toss well. Serves 6.

1 serving: 312 Calories; 3.5 g Total Fat (0.5 g Sat., 43.9 mg Cholesterol); 285 mg Sodium; 25 g Protein; 43 g Carbohydrate; 3 g Dietary Fiber

Pictured on page 36.

Orzo Crust Pizza

A unique pizza using orzo pasta as the crust.

Orzo (very small pasta)	1 cup	250 mL
Boiling water	4 cups	1 L
Salt	1 tsp.	5 mL
Frozen egg product, thawed	6 tbsp.	100 mL
Grated light Parmesan cheese product	2 tbsp.	30 mL
Parsley flakes	2 tsp.	10 mL
Easy Spicy Tomato Sauce, page 110 (or commercial meatless spaghetti sauce)	1½ cups	375 mL
Lean ground chicken (or beef)	½ lb.	225 g
Seasoning salt	½ tsp.	2 mL
Pepper	¼ tsp.	1 mL
Dried whole oregano	½ tsp.	2 mL
Medium green or red pepper, cut into rings	1	1
Medium red onion, thinly sliced	½	½
Chopped fresh mushrooms	⅔ cup	150 mL
Grated part-skim mozzarella cheese	1 cup	250 mL

Cook orzo in boiling water and salt in large saucepan for 12 to 15 minutes, stirring occasionally, until tender but firm. Drain. Return to saucepan.

Combine egg product, Parmesan cheese and parsley in small bowl. Mix. Pour over hot pasta. Toss well. Press in greased 12 inch (30 cm) deep dish pizza pan, forming a crust. Spread tomato sauce over top almost to edges.

Scramble-fry ground chicken, breaking up any large chunks, in medium non-stick skillet until no longer pink. Drain. Add seasoning salt, pepper and oregano. Stir.

Scatter chicken over tomato sauce. Cover with green pepper, onion and mushrooms. Sprinkle mozzarella cheese over top. Bake in 400°F (205°C) oven for 20 minutes until cheese is melted and edges are golden. Cuts into 8 pieces.

1 piece: 223 Calories; 4.6 g Total Fat (2 g Sat., 27.8 mg Cholesterol); 314 mg Sodium; 16 g Protein; 29 g Carbohydrate; 2 g Dietary Fiber

Pictured on page 35.

Curried Chicken Casserole

Mild curry flavor. Only 25 minutes to prepare and assemble.

Penne (medium tube pasta), 6 oz. (170 g)	2 cups	500 mL
Boiling water	2 qts.	2 L
Salt	2 tsp.	10 mL
Boneless, skinless chicken breast halves (about 3), cut into bite-size pieces	¾ lb.	340 g
Olive oil	1 tsp.	5 mL
Sun-dried tomato pesto	1 tbsp.	15 mL
Chopped onion	1 cup	250 mL
Garlic cloves, minced	2	2
Curry paste (available in ethnic section of grocery stores)	1 tsp.	5 mL
White (or alcohol-free white) wine	⅓ cup	75 mL
Water	⅓ cup	75 mL
Chicken bouillon powder	1 tsp.	5 mL
Skim evaporated milk	1 cup	250 mL
Cornstarch	2 tsp.	10 mL
Diced tomato	1 cup	250 mL
Coarse dry bread crumbs	⅓ cup	75 mL
Paprika, sprinkle		

Cook pasta in boiling water and salt in Dutch oven for 7 to 8 minutes, stirring occasionally. Pasta should still be undercooked and quite firm. Drain.

Sauté chicken in oil in large non-stick skillet for about 5 minutes until chicken is golden. Remove to bowl.

Heat pesto in same skillet. Add onion, garlic and curry paste. Sauté for 4 minutes until onion is soft. Stir in wine, water and bouillon powder. Bring to a boil. Add chicken. Cover. Simmer for 5 minutes.

Combine evaporated milk and cornstarch. Mix well. Add to curry mixture. Stir until boiling and slightly thickened. Stir in pasta. Place in greased 1½ quart (1.5 L) casserole dish.

Cover with tomato and bread crumbs. Sprinkle with paprika. Bake, uncovered, in 350°F (175°C) oven for 30 to 40 minutes until hot. Serves 4.

1 serving: 413 Calories; 5.2 g Total Fat (0.9 g Sat., 51.9 mg Cholesterol); 375 mg Sodium; 33 g Protein; 54 g Carbohydrate; 2 g Dietary Fiber

Chicken Dishes

Chicken And Asparagus Pasta

Leeks look like giant scallions. The leek is related to onion and garlic, although its aroma and flavor are milder.

Ditali (small or medium pasta), 10 oz. (285 g)	2½ cups	625 mL
Boiling water	2½ qts.	2.5 L
Salt	2½ tsp.	12 mL
Water	¾ cup	175 mL
White (or alcohol-free white) wine	¼ cup	60 mL
Chicken bouillon powder	2 tsp.	10 mL
Medium leek, thinly sliced (see Tip, page 131)	1	1
Fresh asparagus, sliced into 1 inch (2.5 cm) lengths, eight 4 inch (10 cm) tips reserved	1 lb.	454 g
Garlic cloves, minced	2	2
Skim evaporated milk	¾ cup	175 mL
All-purpose flour	2 tbsp.	30 mL
Diced cooked chicken	2 cups	500 mL
Grated light Parmesan cheese product	2 tbsp.	30 mL

Cook pasta in boiling water and salt in Dutch oven for 9 minutes, stirring occasionally, until tender but firm. Drain.

Heat water, wine and bouillon powder in medium saucepan until boiling. Add leek, asparagus (without reserved tips) and garlic. Stir. Cover. Simmer for 10 minutes. Remove cover. Lay reserved asparagus tips over top. Cover. Cook for 5 minutes until asparagus tips are bright green. Remove tips carefully with slotted spoon and reserve.

Stir evaporated milk and flour together until smooth. Stir into asparagus mixture. Stir until boiling and thickened. Stir in chicken. Add pasta. Mix. Turn into greased 3 quart (3 L) casserole dish. Arrange cooked asparagus tips over top in a pinwheel design. Sprinkle with Parmesan cheese. Cover. Bake in 350°F (175°C) oven for 25 to 30 minutes until hot and bubbling. Serves 6.

1 serving: 341 Calories; 3.3 g Total Fat (0.9 g Sat., 44.7 mg Cholesterol); 340 mg Sodium; 28 g Protein; 48 g Carbohydrate; 3 g Dietary Fiber

Pictured on page 18.

Variation: Substitute ½ cup (125 mL) grated light Cheddar cheese for Parmesan cheese.

Warm Fruit And Pasta

*A beautiful orange zest aroma. Wonderful, refreshing flavor. Tailor
to your own taste buds by adding your favorite dried fruit.*

Juice of 1 large orange		
Prepared orange juice	1 cup	250 mL
Granulated sugar	¼ cup	60 mL
Cornstarch	4 tsp.	20 mL
Salt, just a pinch		
Dried apricots, chopped	4	4
Golden raisins	¼ cup	60 mL
Dried cherries (or other dried fruit), chopped	¼ cup	60 mL
Finely grated peel of 1 large orange, divided		
Angel hair (very thin string) pasta (capellini)	6 oz.	170 g
Boiling water	2 qts.	2 L
Granulated sugar	¼ cup	60 mL
Salt, just a pinch		
Frozen egg product, thawed	6 tbsp.	100 mL
Finely chopped toasted pecans (or walnuts or hazelnuts)	1 tbsp.	15 mL
Hazelnut (or almond) flavored liqueur	1 tbsp.	15 mL

Combine both orange juices in small saucepan. Combine first amount of sugar, cornstarch and salt in small cup. Whisk into orange juice.

Add apricots, raisins, cherries and ½ of orange peel. Bring to a boil. Reduce heat and simmer for 5 minutes.

Cook pasta in boiling water, second amounts of sugar and salt in Dutch oven for 5 to 6 minutes, stirring occasionally, until tender but firm. Drain. Rinse with hot water. Drain. Keep warm.

Add 2 tbsp. (30 mL) hot orange mixture to egg product in small cup. Stir until smooth. Whisk into hot orange mixture. Whisk until boiling and thickened. Remove from heat.

Stir in pecans and liqueur. Pour over pasta on individual plates. Garnish with remaining orange peel. Makes 4 cups (1 L).

½ cup (125 mL): 185 Calories; 1.7 g Total Fat (0.4 g Sat., 0.3 mg Cholesterol); 71 mg Sodium; 5 g Protein; 40 g Carbohydrate; 3 g Dietary Fiber

Chocolate Cheese Manicotti

The manicotti can be cut in half before filling to serve 12. A very rich dessert.

Manicotti shells	6	6
Boiling water	3 qts.	3 L
Salt	½ tsp.	2 mL
White Crème de Cacao liqueur	3 tbsp.	50 mL
Envelope unflavored gelatin	1 × ¼ oz.	1 × 7 g
Non-fat creamed cottage cheese	1½ cups	375 mL
Non-fat spreadable cream cheese	8 oz.	225 g
Granulated sugar	⅓ cup	75 mL
Bittersweet chocolate baking squares, coarsely chopped	2 × 1 oz.	2 × 28 g
Toasted sliced hazelnuts	2 tbsp.	30 mL
Frozen sweetened raspberries in syrup, thawed, syrup reserved	15 oz.	425 g
Cornstarch	1 tbsp.	15 mL

Cook pasta in boiling water and salt in Dutch oven for about 20 minutes, stirring occasionally, until tender but firm. Drain. Rinse with cold water until cool. Drain. Let stand on paper towel until dry.

Place liqueur in small bowl. Sprinkle gelatin over top. Let stand for 5 minutes. Stir. Microwave on medium (50%) for about 45 seconds until gelatin is dissolved. Cool.

Combine cottage cheese, cream cheese and sugar in blender. Process until almost smooth. Add gelatin mixture. Process. Fold the chocolate and hazelnuts into the cottage cheese mixture. Cover. Chill for about 45 minutes. Makes 3 cups (750 mL) filling. Spoon or pipe ½ cup (125 mL) filling into each shell. Cover. Chill for at least 2 hours.

Combine raspberry syrup and cornstarch in small saucepan. Heat, stirring occasionally, until boiling and thickened. Cool slightly. Add to raspberries in separate bowl. Stir. Chill until cool. Drizzle over filled shells. Makes 6 manicotti.

1 filled manicotti: 340 Calories; 8.2 g Total Fat (3.9 g Sat., 1.2 mg Cholesterol); 122 mg Sodium; 18 g Protein; 51 g Carbohydrate; 5 g Dietary Fiber

Pictured on the front cover.

Peach Layered Dessert

A peach and cinnamon-flavored round dessert. A bit
time-consuming but very easy and worth the effort!

Skim milk	2 cups	500 mL
Vanilla custard powder	1/4 cup	60 mL
Granulated sugar	3 tbsp.	50 mL
Skim evaporated milk	1/2 cup	125 mL
Almond flavoring	1/2 tsp.	2 mL
Prepared Egg Pasta Dough, page 87 (1/2 of recipe), see Note	3/4 lb.	340 g
Brown sugar, packed	2 tbsp.	30 mL
Ground cinnamon	1/4 tsp.	1 mL
All-purpose flour	2 tsp.	10 mL
Canned peach halves, slightly drained (fruit should still be quite moist), cut into thin slices	28 oz.	796 mL
Slivered almonds, toasted	2 tbsp.	30 mL

Heat milk in medium saucepan until very hot but not boiling. Combine custard powder, granulated sugar and evaporated milk in small bowl. Mix until smooth. Gradually add to hot milk, stirring constantly, until boiling and thickened. Stir in almond flavoring. Lay plastic wrap on surface of custard to prevent skin from forming. Cool slightly.

Divide rested dough into 3 pieces. Roll out each piece into very thin 8 inch (20 cm) circle. Cover with damp cloth.

Combine brown sugar, cinnamon and flour in small cup.

Layer the following in order given in lightly greased 8 inch (20 cm) springform pan:

1. 1/3 of peach slices
2. 1/3 of brown sugar mixture
3. 1/2 cup (125 mL) custard
4. 1 pasta circle
5. 1/3 of peach slices
6. 1/3 of brown sugar mixture
7. 2/3 cup (150 mL) custard
8. 1 pasta circle
9. 2/3 cup (150 mL) custard
10. 1 pasta circle
11. 1/3 of peach slices
12. 1/3 of brown sugar mixture
13. 2/3 cup (150 mL) custard

(continued on next page)

Sprinkle with almonds. Bake, uncovered, in 350°F (175°C) oven for 40 minutes until set. Cuts into 8 wedges.

1 wedge: 235 Calories; 1.7 g Total Fat (0.3 g Sat., 1.8 mg Cholesterol); 277 mg Sodium; 9 g Protein; 47 g Carbohydrate; 2 g Dietary Fiber

Pictured on page 71.

Note: Lemon Pepper Pasta Dough, page 84, or Basic Pasta Dough, page 86, can be substituted.

Ambrosia Dessert

This dessert is best eaten within three hours. Creamy white and very fruity.

Orzo (very small pasta)	½ cup	125 mL
Boiling water	2 cups	500 mL
Salt	½ tsp.	2 mL
Canned fruit cocktail, with juice	14 oz.	398 mL
Miniature marshmallows	2 cups	500 mL
Maraschino cherries, drained and cut into quarters	5	5
Small banana, diced	1	1
Envelope dessert topping (not prepared)	1	1
Skim milk	⅓ cup	75 mL
Almond (or vanilla) flavoring	½ tsp.	2 mL
Sliced almonds, toasted (optional)	2 tbsp.	30 mL

Cook pasta in boiling water and salt in medium saucepan for about 10 minutes, stirring occasionally, until tender but firm. Drain. Rinse with cold water. Drain.

Combine fruit cocktail, marshmallows, cherries and banana in large bowl. Stir in pasta. Cover. Chill for 2 hours until juice is absorbed.

Beat dessert topping, milk and almond flavoring together in small bowl on high for about 2 minutes until very stiff. Fold topping into fruit mixture.

Sprinkle with almonds before serving. Makes 6 cups (1.5 L).

½ cup (125 mL): 112 Calories; 1.6 g Total Fat (1.3 g Sat., 0.2 mg Cholesterol); 17 mg Sodium; 2 g Protein; 23 g Carbohydrate; 1 g Dietary Fiber

Pictured on page 90.

Layered Salmon "Torte"

This is an attractive change from the regular lasagne shape. Creamy texture.

SALMON SAUCE

Finely chopped onion	1 cup	250 mL
Finely chopped celery	1/2 cup	125 mL
Small garlic clove, minced	1	1
Finely chopped green or red pepper	1/2 cup	125 mL
Tub margarine	2 tsp.	10 mL
White (or alcohol-free white) wine	2 tbsp.	30 mL
Canned crushed tomatoes	14 oz.	398 mL
Chili sauce	1/3 cup	75 mL
Chopped fresh parsley (or 2 tsp., 10 mL, dried)	2 tbsp.	30 mL
Granulated sugar	1/2 tsp.	2 mL
Dried thyme	1/2 tsp.	2 mL
Flaked poached salmon (see Note)	2 cups	500 mL

CHEESE SAUCE

Skim evaporated milk	1 cup	250 mL
All-purpose flour	1/4 cup	60 mL
Grated light Cheddar cheese	1 cup	250 mL
Non-fat creamed cottage cheese	1 cup	250 mL
Frozen egg product, thawed	6 tbsp.	100 mL
Salt	1/2 tsp.	2 mL
Lasagne noodles	9	9
Boiling water	4 qts.	4 L
Salt	4 tsp.	20 mL

Paprika, sprinkle

Salmon Sauce: Sauté onion, celery, garlic and green pepper in margarine in large non-stick skillet until onion is soft. Stir in wine. Simmer, covered, for about 3 minutes. Stir in tomato, chili sauce, parsley, sugar and thyme. Simmer, partially covered, for 10 minutes. Remove from heat. Reserve 1/4 cup (60 mL). Stir salmon into remaining sauce. Makes 3²/₃ cups (900 mL) sauce.

Cheese Sauce: Whisk evaporated milk into flour in medium saucepan until smooth. Cook, stirring constantly, until boiling and thickened. Remove from heat. Stir in Cheddar cheese until melted. Combine cottage cheese, egg product and salt in small bowl. Stir into cheese sauce until combined. Makes 2²/₃ cups (650 mL) sauce.

Cook pasta in boiling water and salt in Dutch oven for 8 to 10 minutes, stirring occasionally, until tender but firm. Drain.

(continued on next page)

Lightly grease 10 inch (25 cm) springform pan and layer casserole as follows:

1. Reserved tomato sauce

2. 3 lasagne noodles, cut to fit

3. 1/2 of salmon sauce

4. 1/3 of cheese sauce

5. 3 lasagne noodles, cut to fit

6. Remaining salmon sauce

7. 1/3 of cheese sauce

8. Remaining 3 lasagne noodles and pieces, arranged in layer to cover

9. Remaining cheese sauce

10. Sprinkle of paprika

Cover tightly with lightly greased foil. Bake in 350°F (175°C) oven for 55 to 60 minutes until hot and starting to bubble. Remove foil. Bake for 10 minutes to set cheese sauce on top. Let stand for 10 minutes before running spatula between casserole and pan side. Remove outside of pan. Cuts into 8 wedges.

1 wedge: 330 Calories; 6.6 g Total Fat (2.7 g Sat., 55.7 mg Cholesterol); 663 mg Sodium; 34 g Protein; 33 g Carbohydrate; 2 g Dietary Fiber

Pictured on page 54.

Note: 2 cans (6 1/2 oz., 185 g, each) flaked salmon, drained, skin and round bones removed, can be substituted for poached salmon.

Paré Pointer
The Boy Scout who does too many good turns is apt to get dizzy.

Creamy Mussels 'N' Pasta

This is a thin sauce that tastes very rich and creamy.

Penne (medium tube pasta), 10 oz. (285 g)	3½ cups	875 mL
Boiling water	4 qts.	4 L
Salt	4 tsp.	20 mL
Large garlic cloves, minced	3	3
Finely chopped onion	½ cup	125 mL
Dried crushed chilies	⅛ tsp.	0.5 mL
Cayenne pepper	¹⁄₁₆ tsp.	0.5 mL
Olive oil	2 tsp.	10 mL
Canned red peppers, drained and finely diced	14 oz.	398 mL
White (or alcohol-free) wine	½ cup	125 mL
Light spreadable cream cheese	2 tbsp.	30 mL
Fresh mussels (about 30), beards removed and scrubbed clean (see Note)	2¼ lbs.	1 kg
Green onions, sliced	2	2
Chopped fresh parsley	2 tbsp.	30 mL

Cook pasta in boiling water and salt in Dutch oven for 10 to 12 minutes, stirring occasionally, until tender but firm. Drain. Rinse with warm water. Drain.

Sauté garlic, onion, chilies and cayenne pepper in oil in large non-stick wok for 2 minutes until onion is soft. Add red pepper. Sauté for 2 minutes.

Stir in wine and cream cheese. Bring to a boil. Add mussels. Cover and simmer for 3 minutes until shells are open. Add pasta, green onion and parsley. Stir gently. Cover. Cook for 1 minute until pasta is warm. Discard any mussels that remain closed. Serve immediately. Serves 4.

1 serving: 395 Calories; 6 g Total Fat (1.4 g Sat., 18.5 mg Cholesterol); 313 mg Sodium; 17 g Protein; 62 g Carbohydrate; 3 g Dietary Fiber

Pictured on page 53.

Note: Before cooking, discard any mussels that are open or remain open when sharply tapped.

Pasta Paella

Paella (pi-AY-yuh) is a Spanish dish named after the special two-handled pan it was originally prepared and served in. Perfect for company.

Boneless, skinless chicken breast halves (about 2), diced into ³/₄ inch (2 cm) pieces	¹/₂ lb.	225 g
Olive oil	1 tsp.	5 mL
Large garlic cloves, minced	3	3
Medium onions, chopped	2	2
Dried crushed chilies	¹/₂ tsp.	2 mL
Olive oil	1 tsp.	5 mL
Medium red peppers, diced	2	2
Canned diced tomatoes, with juice	28 oz.	796 mL
Condensed chicken broth	10 oz.	284 mL
Hot water	2 cups	500 mL
Reserved clam juice		
Salt	1 tsp.	5 mL
Coarsely ground pepper	¹/₂ tsp.	2 mL
Crushed saffron threads	¹/₄ tsp.	1 mL
Dried whole oregano	¹/₄ tsp.	1 mL
Uncooked orzo (very small pasta)	2 cups	500 mL
Canned baby clams, drained, juice reserved	5 oz.	142 g
Fresh mussels (about 15), beards removed and scrubbed clean (see Note)	1 lb.	454 g
Medium cooked shrimp	5 oz.	140 g
Frozen peas, thawed	1 cup	250 mL

Sauté chicken in first amount of oil in large non-stick skillet or Dutch oven until lightly golden. Remove to small bowl.

Sauté garlic, onion and chilies in second amount of oil for 3 minutes until onion is soft. Add red pepper. Sauté for 2 minutes.

Add tomato, chicken broth, hot water, reserved clam juice, salt, pepper, saffron and oregano. Bring to a boil.

Add orzo and chicken. Cover. Simmer for 15 minutes.

Add clams and mussels. Cover. Simmer for 3 minutes. Add shrimp and peas. Stir. Cover. Simmer for about 3 minutes until hot. Discard any mussels that remain closed. Serves 8.

1 serving: 382 Calories; 4 g Total Fat (0.7 g Sat., 62.1 mg Cholesterol); 901 mg Sodium; 27 g Protein; 59 g Carbohydrate; 4 g Dietary Fiber

Pictured on page 71.

Note: Before cooking, discard any mussels that are open or remain open when sharply tapped.

Linguine With Smoked Salmon And Olives

Easy and quick to prepare. Garlic and wine flavors complement the salmon.

Garlic clove, minced	1	1
Finely chopped onion	¼ cup	60 mL
Olive oil	1 tsp.	5 mL
Smoked salmon, diced or cut into strips	5 oz.	140 g
Water	¼ cup	60 mL
White (or alcohol-free white) wine	¼ cup	60 mL
Chopped fresh parsley (or 1 tsp., 5 mL, dried)	1 tbsp.	15 mL
Chopped fresh dill (or ½ tsp., 2 mL, dried)	1½ tsp.	7 mL
Seafood (or vegetable) bouillon powder	½ tsp.	2 mL
Freshly ground pepper, sprinkle		
Dried crushed chilies, sprinkle		
Chopped ripe pitted olives	1 tbsp.	15 mL
Linguine (flat string pasta)	8 oz.	225 g
Boiling water	2 qts.	2 L
Salt	2 tsp.	10 mL

Sauté garlic and onion in oil in medium skillet for about 2 minutes until onion is soft.

Stir in next 9 ingredients. Cover. Keep warm over low.

Cook pasta in boiling water and salt in Dutch oven for 8 to 10 minutes, stirring occasionally, until tender but firm. Drain. Return to Dutch oven. Pour sauce over. Toss to coat. Serve immediately. Serves 4.

1 serving: 280 Calories; 3.8 g Total Fat (0.7 g Sat., 8.1 mg Cholesterol); 799 mg Sodium; 14 g Protein; 44 g Carbohydrate; 2 g Dietary Fiber

Pictured on page 53.

1. Linguine With Smoked Salmon And Olives, above
2. Creamy Mussels 'N' Pasta, page 50
3. Garlic Shrimp And Vegetable Sauce, page 112
4. Cannelloni St. Jacques, page 140

Props Courtesy Of: Stokes
The Basket House

Angel Hair Scampi

Refreshing garlic, lemon and wine-flavored sauce.

Angel hair (very thin string) pasta (capellini)	8 oz.	225 g
Boiling water	2 qts.	2 L
Salt	2 tsp.	10 mL
Garlic cloves, finely chopped	3	3
Olive oil	1 tsp.	5 mL
Water	1 cup	250 mL
Seafood bouillon powder	1 tbsp.	15 mL
Granulated sugar	1½ tbsp.	25 mL
White (or alcohol-free) wine	½ cup	125 mL
Cornstarch	2 tbsp.	30 mL
Grated lemon peel	4 tsp.	20 mL
Finely sliced fresh chive	2 tbsp.	30 mL
Cooked prawns, shelled and deveined	12 oz.	340 g
Freshly ground pepper, sprinkle		

Cook pasta in boiling water and salt in Dutch oven for 5 minutes, stirring occasionally, until tender but firm. Drain. Return to Dutch oven. Keep warm.

Sauté garlic in oil in medium non-stick skillet until soft. Add water, bouillon powder and sugar. Heat, uncovered, until simmering.

Combine wine and cornstarch in small cup. Stir into garlic mixture. Stir until boiling and slightly thickened. Remove from heat.

Stir in lemon peel, chive and prawns. Heat for 1 minute. Pour over pasta. Toss. Sprinkle with pepper. Serves 4.

1 serving: 371 Calories; 3.2 g Total Fat (0.6 g Sat., 166 mg Cholesterol); 643 mg Sodium; 26 g Protein; 53 g Carbohydrate; 2 g Dietary Fiber

Pictured on page 72.

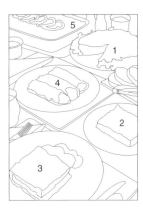

1. Layered Salmon "Torte", page 48
2. Seafood Lasagne, page 56
3. Pastitsio, page 24
4. Leek And Spinach Manicotti, page 138
5. Vegetable Lasagne, page 68

Props Courtesy Of: Eaton's
Stokes
The Bay

Seafood Lasagne

You will love the aroma while this casserole is baking! Rich sauce loaded with seafood.

Finely chopped onion	1¹/₂ cups	375 mL
Garlic clove, minced	1	1
Tub margarine	2 tsp.	10 mL
White (or alcohol-free white) wine	¹/₂ cup	125 mL
All-purpose flour	¹/₃ cup	75 mL
Cornstarch	2 tbsp.	30 mL
Seafood bouillon powder	4 tsp.	20 mL
Parsley flakes	1 tbsp.	15 mL
Onion powder	¹/₂ tsp.	2 mL
Garlic powder	¹/₄ tsp.	1 mL
Skim evaporated milk	13¹/₂ oz.	385 mL
Skim milk	2¹/₂ cups	625 mL
Hot pepper sauce	¹/₄ tsp.	1 mL
Cooked small shrimp, peeled and deveined	8 oz.	225 g
Cooked small scallops (see Note)	8 oz.	225 g
Canned crabmeat, drained and cartilage removed	2 x 4 oz.	2 x 113 g
Spinach lasagne noodles	9	9
Boiling water	4 qts.	4 L
Salt	4 tsp.	20 mL
Grated part-skim mozzarella cheese	¹/₃ cup	75 mL
Grated light Cheddar cheese	¹/₃ cup	75 mL

Sauté onion and garlic in margarine in medium skillet for 3 minutes until just starting to become soft. Stir in wine. Cook, uncovered, for 10 minutes until liquid is evaporated and onion is very soft.

Stir next 6 ingredients together in medium saucepan. Slowly whisk in both milks until smooth. Cook, stirring constantly, until boiling and thickened. Stir in hot pepper sauce and onion mixture.

Remove ¹/₂ cup (125 mL) sauce. Spread in bottom of lightly greased 9 x 13 inch (22 x 33 cm) baking dish. In each of 3 small bowls, combine ¹/₃ (about 2 cups, 500 mL) of remaining sauce with shrimp, ¹/₃ (about 2 cups, 500 mL) with scallops and ¹/₃ (about 2 cups, 500 mL) with crabmeat.

Cook lasagne noodles in boiling water and salt in Dutch oven for 10 minutes, stirring occasionally, until just firm. Drain and rinse under cold water. Place 3 noodles in layer over sauce in baking dish. Cover with shrimp sauce. Repeat with layer of 3 noodles and layer of scallop sauce. Repeat with remaining 3 noodles and remaining crab sauce.

Top with both cheeses. Cover with lightly greased foil. Bake in 350°F (175°C) oven for 45 minutes. Remove foil. Bake, uncovered, for 10 to 15 minutes to brown cheese. Let stand for 15 minutes to set before cutting. Serves 8.

(continued on next page)

Fish & Seafood Dishes

1 serving: 285 Calories; 3.8 g Total Fat (1.5 g Sat., 32.5 mg Cholesterol); 702 mg Sodium; 22 g Protein; 37 g Carbohydrate; 3 g Dietary Fiber

Pictured on page 54.

Note: To poach scallops, combine ¹/₃ cup (75 mL) water, ¹/₃ cup (75 mL) white (or alcohol-free white) wine and 1 bay leaf in small saucepan. Simmer scallops for 1 to 2 minutes until just opaque. Drain. Discard bay leaf.

Easy Curry Seafood

Just enough curry to complement the delicate seafood flavor.

Large (not jumbo) shell pasta (8 oz., 225 g)	3 cups	750 mL
Boiling water	3 qts.	3 L
Salt	1 tbsp.	15 mL
Diet tub margarine	1 tbsp.	15 mL
Curry paste (available in ethnic section of grocery stores)	1¹/₂ tsp.	7 mL
All-purpose flour	2 tbsp.	30 mL
Skim evaporated milk	13¹/₂ oz.	385 mL
Skim milk	¹/₂ cup	125 mL
Seafood (or chicken) bouillon powder	1 tsp.	5 mL
Non-fat spreadable cream cheese	¹/₄ cup	60 mL
Variety of cooked seafood, cut into bite-size pieces (14 oz., 395 g)	3 cups	750 mL
Chopped pimiento (or coarse dry bread crumbs), for garnish (optional)		

Cook pasta in boiling water and salt in Dutch oven for 8 to 10 minutes, stirring occasionally, until tender but firm. Drain. Return to Dutch oven to keep warm.

Melt margarine and curry paste in large saucepan. Add flour. Mix well. Slowly whisk in both milks until smooth. Cook, stirring constantly, until boiling and slightly thickened. Stir in bouillon powder and cream cheese.

Stir in seafood. Pour over pasta and fold in. Place in greased 2 quart (2 L) casserole dish. Garnish with pimiento. Cover. Bake in 350°F (175°C) oven for 30 minutes until hot and bubbling. Serves 4.

1 serving: 451 Calories; 4.3 g Total Fat (0.8 g Sat., 107.9 mg Cholesterol); 771 mg Sodium; 39 g Protein; 62 g Carbohydrate; 2 g Dietary Fiber

Asian Fish Fry

Hoisin (HOY-sihn) sauce is also called Peking sauce. It is widely used in Chinese cooking. It is available in Asian markets or at many large supermarkets.

Hoisin sauce	1/4 cup	60 mL
Liquid honey	2 tbsp.	30 mL
Dried crushed chilies	1/4 - 1/2 tsp.	1-2 mL
Ground coriander	1/8 tsp.	0.5 mL
Rice vinegar	2 tbsp.	30 mL
Cornstarch	1 tbsp.	15 mL
Sesame oil	1 tsp.	5 mL
Boneless cod fillets, cut into 1 1/2 inch (3.8 cm) chunks	1 lb.	454 g
Sesame oil	1 tsp.	5 mL
Large onion, sliced lengthwise into thin wedges	1	1
Large green, red, orange or yellow pepper, cut into slivers	1	1
Coarsely shredded green cabbage	2 cups	500 mL
Toasted sesame seeds (optional)	2 tsp.	10 mL
Vermicelli (thin string pasta), broken into thirds	8 oz.	225 g
Boiling water	2 qts.	2 L
Salt	2 tsp.	10 mL

Combine first 6 ingredients in small bowl.

Heat first amount of oil in large non-stick skillet or wok. Add cod. Cook for 2 minutes. Turn pieces over gently to cook other side for 2 minutes until fish flakes easily. Remove to plate.

Heat second amount of oil in same skillet. Sauté onion, green pepper and cabbage for 5 minutes until tender-crisp. Add hoisin sauce mixture. Heat, stirring constantly, until boiling and slightly thickened. Add cod. Stir gently to coat with sauce. Sprinkle with sesame seeds. Makes 5 cups (1.25 L).

Cook pasta in boiling water and salt in Dutch oven for 5 to 6 minutes, stirring occasionally, until tender but firm. Drain. Place in serving dish. Arrange fish and sauce over top. Serves 6.

1 serving: 310 Calories; 6.2 g Total Fat (1.1 g Sat., 32.5 mg Cholesterol); 528 mg Sodium; 17 g Protein; 47 g Carbohydrate; 3 g Dietary Fiber

Pictured on page 89.

Mushroom And Asparagus Pasta

For this dish use any kind of medium or string pasta you have in your cupboard.

Asparagus, cut on the diagonal into 1 inch (2.5 cm) lengths	1 lb.	454 g
Water	2 tbsp.	30 mL
Chopped onion	½ cup	125 mL
Garlic clove, minced	1	1
Tub margarine	1 tsp.	5 mL
Sliced fresh mushrooms	3 cups	750 mL
Salt	¾ tsp.	4 mL
Freshly ground pepper, sprinkle		
Frozen egg product, thawed	6 tbsp.	100 mL
Skim evaporated milk	½ cup	125 mL
Grated light Parmesan cheese product	2 tbsp.	30 mL
Penne (medium tube pasta), 10 oz. (285 g)	3½ cups	875 ml
Boiling water	4 qts.	4 L
Salt	4 tsp.	20 mL
Toasted pine nuts, coarsely chopped (optional)	2 tsp.	10 mL

Place asparagus and water in 1 quart (1 L) microwave-safe casserole dish. Cover. Microwave on high (100%) for about 5 minutes until just tender. Drain. Keep warm.

Sauté onion and garlic in margarine in medium non-stick skillet for 2 minutes. Add mushrooms. Sauté for about 4 minutes. Cook until liquid is evaporated and mushrooms are golden. Add first amount of salt and pepper. Stir. Keep warm.

Beat egg product, evaporated milk and cheese together in small bowl.

Cook pasta in boiling water and second amount of salt in Dutch oven for 8 to 10 minutes, stirring occasionally, until tender but firm. Drain. Return pasta to Dutch oven. Add milk mixture. Stir. Add asparagus, mushroom mixture and pine nuts. Mix well until liquid is absorbed. Serve immediately. Serves 8.

1 serving: 182 Calories; 1.4 g Total Fat (0.3 g Sat., 1.2 mg Cholesterol); 334 mg Sodium; 10 g Protein; 33 g Carbohydrate; 2 g Dietary Fiber

 Fresh herbs and vegetables add lots of flavor to pasta dishes, without adding fat. Try vitamin and flavor-laden red, yellow, green or orange peppers in a sauce instead of meat or cheese.

Zucchini Pesto Sauté

Beautiful green sauce that coats the pasta nicely.

Medium zucchini, with peel, grated	4	4
Salt	2 tsp.	10 mL
Basil Pesto, page 78 (or commercial)	2 tbsp.	30 mL
Garlic cloves, minced	3	3
Spaghettini (thin string pasta), broken into thirds	8 oz.	225 g
Boiling water	2 qts.	2 L
Olive oil, divided	2 tsp.	10 mL
Freshly ground pepper, sprinkle		
Grated light Parmesan cheese product	2 tbsp.	30 mL

Toss zucchini with salt in large colander over sink or large bowl to catch drips. Let stand for 15 minutes. Drain liquid by squeezing or by pushing through cheesecloth. Place drained and squeezed zucchini in medium bowl and combine well with pesto and garlic.

Cook pasta in boiling water (no salt added) for 5 to 6 minutes in large saucepan or Dutch oven, stirring occasionally, until tender but firm. Drain. Rinse with hot water. Place in pasta bowl.

Heat a large non-stick skillet or wok until hot. Add 1 tsp. (5 mL) oil and then ¹/₂ of zucchini mixture. Stir-fry for 3 to 4 minutes, stirring constantly, separating zucchini mixture. Remove zucchini mixture to pasta bowl. Repeat with remaining oil and zucchini mixture.

Toss zucchini mixture with pasta. Sprinkle with pepper and Parmesan cheese. Serve immediately. Serves 4.

1 serving: 301 Calories; 7.5 g Total Fat (1.4 g Sat., 1.9 mg Cholesterol); 262 mg Sodium; 11 g Protein; 48 g Carbohydrate; 4 g Dietary Fiber

Pictured on page 126.

 Freeze homemade Basil Pesto, page 78, in ice-cube trays. Once the cubes have frozen, transfer to a sealable plastic freezer bag. Thaw individual cubes as needed.

Warm Pepper And Lentil Medley

Lots of zip and texture in this combination.
Serve warm as a side dish, or cold as a salad.

Large red pepper	1	1
Water	¼ cup	60 mL
Lemon juice	2 tbsp.	30 mL
Garlic clove, crushed	1	1
Olive oil	2 tsp.	10 mL
Hot pepper sauce	1 tsp.	5 mL
Freshly ground pepper, sprinkle		
Green lentils	¼ cup	60 mL
Boiling water	4 cups	1 L
Salt	1 tsp.	5 mL
Bay leaves	5	5
Uncooked very small bow tie (or shell) pasta	1 cup	250 mL
Large celery rib, thinly sliced	1	1
Finely chopped red onion	¼ cup	60 mL
Coarsely shredded carrot	¼ cup	60 mL

Place red pepper on baking sheet with sides. Broil, turning often, for 15 to 20 minutes until skin is blackened. Place in small bowl. Cover with plastic wrap. Cool for 10 minutes or until cool enough to handle. Peel skin from pepper, discarding seeds and membrane, and reserving any liquid. Dice roasted pepper and place in medium bowl.

Strain reserved liquid into small bowl. Add next 6 ingredients. Whisk together well.

Cook lentils in boiling water, second amount of salt and bay leaves in large saucepan for 10 to 12 minutes, stirring occasionally. Add pasta. Simmer, uncovered, stirring frequently, for about 8 minutes until pasta is tender. Cover if liquid seems to be disappearing too quickly. Discard bay leaves.

Pour lentil mixture into bowl with red pepper. Add celery, red onion and carrot. Add dressing. Stir together. Serves 4.

1 serving: 185 Calories; 2.9 g Total Fat (0.4 g Sat., 0 mg Cholesterol); 694 mg Sodium; 8 g Protein; 33 g Carbohydrate; 3 g Dietary Fiber

Pictured on page 18.

Thai Rice Noodles

You can find rice vermicelli (or rice stick noodles) at large grocery stores or Asian specialty stores.

Smooth peanut butter	2 tbsp.	30 mL
Low-sodium soy sauce	2 tbsp.	30 mL
Non-fat spreadable cream cheese	2 tbsp.	30 mL
Liquid honey	1 tsp.	5 mL
Dried crushed chilies	1/2 tsp.	2 mL
Grated gingerroot	1 tsp.	5 mL
Garlic clove, minced	1	1
Cornstarch	1 tbsp.	15 mL
Water	1 tbsp.	15 mL
Water	2/3 cup	150 mL
Vegetable bouillon powder	1 tsp.	5 mL
Medium carrot, cut julienne	1	1
Medium red pepper, quartered and thinly sliced	1	1
Fresh bean sprouts (5 oz., 140 g)	2 cups	500 mL
Green onions, sliced twice lengthwise and cut into 4 inch (10 cm) pieces	2	2
Rice vermicelli (thin string pasta), broken into thirds	8 oz.	225 g
Boiling water	2 qts.	2 L
Chopped toasted peanuts	2 tbsp.	30 mL

Combine first 9 ingredients in small bowl.

Heat second amount of water and bouillon powder in large non-stick skillet until boiling. Add carrot. Simmer, uncovered, for 2 minutes.

Stir in red pepper, bean sprouts and green onion. Cover. Cook for 2 minutes. Make a well in center of bean sprout mixture. Pour peanut butter mixture into well. Mix well. Heat until thickened.

Cook rice noodles in boiling water in Dutch oven for 1 minute. Drain and rinse. Toss with bean sprout mixture. Sprinkle with peanuts. Serve immediately. Serves 4.

1 serving: 327 Calories; 4.8 g Total Fat (0.9 g Sat., 0.1 mg Cholesterol); 511 mg Sodium; 9 g Protein; 56 g Carbohydrate; 4 g Dietary Fiber

Pictured on page 71.

 Always use a warm serving dish for pasta. An easy way to warm even delicate china is to pour hot water into the dish and let stand for a few minutes to absorb heat. Empty the dish, wipe dry, and quickly add hot pasta and sauce. Serve immediately.

Pasta And Ceci

Ceci (CHEH-chee) is the Italian word for "chick pea."

Small onion, diced	1	1
Large garlic clove, minced	1	1
Olive oil	1 tsp.	5 mL
Canned chick peas (garbanzo beans), with liquid	19 oz.	540 mL
Celery rib, diced	1	1
Medium carrot, diced	1	1
Chopped fresh parsley, packed (or 1 tbsp., 15 mL, dried)	1/4 cup	60 mL
Canned plum tomatoes, with juice, broken up	14 oz.	398 mL
Bay leaf	1	1
Salt	1/4 tsp.	1 mL
Ground cumin (optional)	1/8 tsp.	0.5 mL
Dried crushed chilies	1/8 tsp.	0.5 mL
Pepper	1/8 tsp.	0.5 mL
Fettuccine (flat string pasta)	8 oz.	225 g
Boiling water	2 qts.	2 L
Salt	2 tsp.	10 mL
Olive oil	1 tsp.	5 mL
Fettuccine (flat string pasta), broken into 1 inch (2.5 cm) lengths	2 oz.	57 g

Sauté onion and garlic in first amount of oil in large non-stick skillet until onion is soft. Add chick peas. Bring to a boil. Add celery, carrot and parsley. Cover. Simmer for 10 minutes until carrot is tender.

Stir in tomato. Add bay leaf, first amount of salt, cumin, chilies and pepper. Stir. Bring to a boil. Simmer, partially covered, for 30 minutes until slightly thickened. Discard bay leaf.

Cook first amount of fettuccine in boiling water and second amount of salt in Dutch oven for 8 to 10 minutes, stirring occasionally, until tender but firm. Drain. Return to Dutch oven. Pour sauce over top. Toss well and keep warm.

Heat second amount of oil in large non-stick skillet. Add second amount of fettuccine. Cook for about 3 minutes, stirring constantly, until golden brown and crisp. Turn out onto paper towel and blot dry. Sprinkle over pasta and sauce. Serve immediately. Serves 4.

1 serving: 482 Calories; 5.4 g Total Fat (0.7 g Sat., 0 mg Cholesterol); 762 mg Sodium; 17 g Protein; 92 g Carbohydrate; 8 g Dietary Fiber

Pictured on page 126.

Herb Pasta With Sun-Dried Tomatoes

A nice spicy sauce. Add as much or as little chilies as you like.

Small to medium herb pasta (any flavor), 8 oz. (225 g)	2 cups	500 mL
Boiling water	2 qts.	2 L
Salt	2 tsp.	10 mL
Garlic clove, minced	1	1
Dried crushed chilies	⅛-¼ tsp.	0.5-1 mL
Green onions, sliced	2	2
Sun-dried tomato halves, chopped (see Note)	4	4
Olive oil	2 tsp.	10 mL
Rosé (or white) wine	⅓ cup	75 mL
Juice of 1 medium orange		
Grated orange peel	2 tsp.	10 mL
Water	⅓ cup	75 mL
Chicken bouillon powder	½ tsp.	2 mL
Tomato paste	1 tbsp.	15 mL
Seeded and diced tomato	2 cups	500 mL
Freshly ground pepper, sprinkle		

Cook pasta in boiling water and salt in Dutch oven for 8 to 10 minutes, stirring occasionally, until tender but firm. Drain. Return to Dutch oven and keep warm.

Sauté garlic, chilies, green onion and sun-dried tomato in large non-stick skillet for 3 minutes.

Add next 6 ingredients. Bring to a boil. Simmer, uncovered, for 2 minutes. Add tomato and pepper. Stir until warm. Pour over warm pasta and toss. Serve immediately. Serves 4.

1 serving: 281 Calories; 3.7 g Total Fat (1 g Sat., 0.1 mg Cholesterol); 99 mg Sodium; 9 g Protein; 50 g Carbohydrate; 3 g Dietary Fiber

Note: Kitchen scissors work well to cut sun-dried tomato halves into small pieces, if too hard to chop.

Paré Pointer

Can you still go out in the country to see a barn dance?

Meatless Dishes

Stephe's Fiery Pasta

Go for the gusto! Add a refreshing chilled salad to help put out the fire.

Ripe large plum tomatoes	6	6
Boiling water, to cover		
Very cold (or ice) water, to cover		
Garlic cloves, minced	3	3
Small red or green chili pepper(s), chopped (see Note)	1-4	1-4
Olive oil	2 tsp.	10 mL
White (or alcohol-free) wine	1/4 cup	60 mL
Salt	1 tsp.	5 mL
Granulated sugar, pinch		
Freshly ground pepper, sprinkle		
Spaghettini (thin string pasta)	8 oz.	225 g
Boiling water	2 qts.	2 L
Salt	2 tsp.	10 mL
Grated light Parmesan cheese product	2 tbsp.	30 mL

Place tomatoes in boiling water in large saucepan for 1 minute. Immediately plunge into very cold water. Remove skins and discard. Dice tomatoes, discarding seeds. Place in small bowl.

Sauté garlic and chili pepper in oil in large non-stick skillet, stirring constantly, for 1 minute. Stir in wine. Bring mixture to a boil. Cook, uncovered, for about 4 minutes until wine is almost evaporated. Stir in tomato, first amount of salt, sugar and pepper. Cook, uncovered, for about 3 minutes just until tomato is heated through.

Cook pasta in boiling water and second amount of salt in large saucepan for 7 to 8 minutes, stirring occasionally, until tender but firm. Drain. Return to saucepan.

Toss pasta with tomato mixture. Sprinkle with Parmesan cheese. Serves 4.

1 serving: 296 Calories; 4.3 g Total Fat (0.8 g Sat., 1.2 mg Cholesterol); 757 mg Sodium; 10 g Protein; 53 g Carbohydrate; 4 g Dietary Fiber

Pictured on page 36.

Note: Small red chili peppers (Scotch Bonnet or Finger Peppers) are the hottest; be careful how many you use. Remove the seeds and veins as they provide even more heat. When chopping chili peppers use gloves, as the caustic oily compounds called capsaicin (kap-SAY-ih-sihn), permeate the skin and can actually cause a burning sensation.

Radiatore With Roasted Pepper Salsa

Silky smooth texture. Roasting the peppers is the trick to this extraordinary dish.
Delicious warm or cold.

Large orange or yellow peppers	2	2
Large red peppers	2	2
Garlic clove, minced	1	1
Olive oil	2 tsp.	10 mL
Non-fat Italian dressing	⅓ cup	75 mL
Balsamic vinegar	1 tbsp.	15 mL
Ripe pitted olives, sliced	6	6
Finely chopped fresh sweet basil	¼ cup	60 mL
Finely chopped fresh parsley	2 tbsp.	30 mL
Salt	½ tsp.	2 mL
Freshly ground pepper, sprinkle		
Radiatore (spiral pasta), 8 oz. (225 g)	2⅔ cups	650 mL
Boiling water	3 qts.	3 L
Salt	1 tbsp.	15 mL
Pine nuts, toasted and chopped (optional)	1 tbsp.	15 mL

Place peppers on baking sheet with sides. Broil, turning often, for 15 to 20 minutes until skin is blackened. Place in small bowl. Cover with plastic wrap for 15 to 20 minutes until cool enough to handle. Peel skin from peppers, reserving any liquid. Strain reserved liquid. Discard seeds and membrane. Cut peppers into long slivers. Place in medium bowl.

Sauté garlic in oil in small saucepan until soft. Remove from heat. Add next 7 ingredients. Add reserved liquid from peppers. Stir. Pour over peppers. Marinate at room temperature for at least 1 hour. At this point, salsa can be refrigerated overnight and brought to room temperature before serving.

Cook pasta in boiling water and second amount of salt in Dutch oven for 8 to 10 minutes, stirring occasionally, until tender but firm. Drain. Return to Dutch oven. Pour salsa over top. Mix well.

Sprinkle with pine nuts. Serves 4.

1 serving: 268 Calories; 4.1 g Total Fat (0.6 g Sat., 0 mg Cholesterol); 639 mg Sodium; 8 g Protein; 50 g Carbohydrate; 3 g Dietary Fiber

Pictured on the front cover.

Perfect Pasta Peppers

Very colorful. Use the same color of peppers or any combination of the four colors.

Orzo (very small pasta)	1 cup	250 mL
Boiling water	2 qts.	2 L
Salt	2 tsp.	10 mL
Basil Pesto, page 78 (or commercial)	1 tbsp.	15 mL
Ripe medium plum tomatoes, diced	2	2
Chopped pitted ripe olives	2 tbsp.	30 mL
Chopped fresh parsley (or 1 tsp., 5 mL, dried)	1 tbsp.	15 mL
Chopped fresh sweet basil (or 1 tsp., 5 mL, dried)	1 tbsp.	15 mL
Capers, rinsed and chopped (optional)	2 tsp.	10 mL
Salt	⅛ tsp.	0.5 mL
Freshly ground pepper, sprinkle		
Medium bell peppers, similar in size and shape	3	3
Grated part-skim mozzarella cheese	½ cup	125 mL
Dry bread crumbs	2 tbsp.	30 mL

Cook pasta in boiling water and first amount of salt in large saucepan for 10 minutes, stirring occasionally. Drain. Return to saucepan. Toss with pesto until coated. Stir in next 7 ingredients.

Cut peppers lengthwise through stem. Remove seeds and ribs from each half. Divide pasta mixture among 6 halves. Arrange in lightly greased shallow baking dish that will hold them all in single layer. Cover tightly with lid or seal with foil. Bake in 400°F (205°C) oven for 30 minutes until peppers are just tender-crisp. Combine mozzarella cheese and bread crumbs in small bowl. Divide mixture among pepper halves. Return to top rack of oven. Bake until cheese is melted and bread crumbs are browned. Serves 6.

1 serving: 224 Calories; 4 g Total Fat (1.4 g Sat., 6.1 mg Cholesterol); 159 mg Sodium; 9 g Protein; 38 g Carbohydrate; 2 g Dietary Fiber

Pictured on page 35.

 tip *Olive oil is high in unsaturated fat and low in saturated fat, so it's a great low-fat alternative to margarine or butter. It does not burn as quickly as margarine or butter, so it allows a nice medium heat for sautéing, or a higher heat for stir-frying. Extra virgin olive oil will lend more flavor than virgin or regular olive oil as it is from the first pressing of the olives.*

Vegetable Lasagne

This is a fabulous lasagne! It takes 1 to 1½ hours to prepare — but it's a real crowd-pleaser.

CREAM SAUCE

Skim evaporated milk	13½ oz.	385 ml
Skim milk	1½ cups	375 mL
All-purpose flour	¼ cup	60 mL
Grated light Parmesan cheese product	3 tbsp.	50 mL
Onion powder	½ tsp.	2 mL
Salt	½ tsp.	2 mL
Garlic powder	¼ tsp.	1 mL

STEWED TOMATO SAUCE

Large onion, finely diced	1	1
Garlic cloves, minced	2	2
Olive oil	2 tsp.	10 mL
Large green pepper, finely diced	1	1
Medium red pepper, finely diced	1	1
Medium yellow pepper, finely diced	1	1
Dried whole oregano	1½ tsp.	7 mL
Dried sweet basil	1 tsp.	5 mL
Granulated sugar	1 tsp.	5 mL
Salt	½ tsp.	2 mL
Pepper	¼ tsp.	1 mL
Canned stewed tomatoes, with juice, chopped	3 x 14 oz.	3 x 398 mL
Tomato sauce	7.5 oz.	213 mL
Medium zucchini, with peel	4	4
Boiling water	3 qts.	3 L
Salt	1 tbsp.	15 mL
Lasagne noodles	12	12
Boiling water	5 qts.	5 L
Salt	1½ tbsp.	25 mL
Grated part-skim mozzarella cheese	¾ cup	175 mL

Cream Sauce: Slowly whisk both milks into flour in medium saucepan until smooth. Cook, stirring frequently, until mixture is boiling and thickened. Remove from heat. Stir in remaining 4 ingredients. Makes 3 cups (750 mL) sauce.

Stewed Tomato Sauce: Sauté onion and garlic in oil for 3 to 4 minutes in large non-stick skillet until soft. Stir in peppers and seasonings. Cook for 2 minutes until pepper is tender-crisp. Add tomato and tomato sauce. Boil, uncovered, for 15 minutes until reduced and thickened. Makes 8 cups (2 L) sauce.

(continued on next page)

Meatless Dishes

Cut zucchini, lengthwise, into ¼ inch (6 mm) slices. Blanch in first amounts of boiling water and salt in Dutch oven for 3 minutes. Drain. Rinse with cold water. Lay on tea towel or paper towel to dry well.

Cook lasagne noodles in second amount of boiling water and second amount of salt in same Dutch oven for 10 minutes, stirring occasionally, until just tender.

Assemble lasagne in lightly greased 9 x 13 inch (22 x 33 cm) baking dish as follows:

1. ½ cup (125 mL) stewed tomato sauce
2. 4 lasagne noodles
3. 2½ cups (625 mL) stewed tomato sauce
4. 1 cup (250 mL) cream sauce
5. ½ of zucchini
6. 4 lasagne noodles
7. 2½ cups (625 mL) stewed tomato sauce
8. 1 cup (250 mL) cream sauce
9. Remaining ½ of zucchini
10. 4 lasagne noodles
11. 2½ cups (625 mL) stewed tomato sauce
12. 1 cup (250 mL) cream sauce
13. All of mozzarella cheese

Cover with lightly greased foil. Bake in 350°F (175°C) oven for 45 minutes. Remove foil. Bake for 10 to 15 minutes until cheese is melted and slightly golden. Let stand, uncovered, for 10 to 15 minutes before cutting. Serves 10.

1 serving: 248 Calories; 3.6 g Total Fat (1.5 g Sat., 8.3 mg Cholesterol); 881 mg Sodium; 14 g Protein; 43 g Carbohydrate; 4 g Dietary Fiber

Pictured on page 54.

Paré Pointer

It really kept her busy watching her husband and her furnace.
When she watched one, the other went out.

Derrick's Peach-Of-A-Pasta Dish

Fast! Fast! Fast! And oh so good!

Angel hair (very thin string) pasta (capellini) or vermicelli (thin string pasta)	6 oz.	170 g
Boiling water	2 qts.	2 L
Salt	2 tsp.	10 mL
Tub margarine	1 tsp.	5 mL
Diced ripe peach or nectarine, unpeeled	1½ cups	375 mL
Diced ripe tomato	1½ cups	375 mL
Brown sugar, packed	1 tsp.	5 mL
Salt	½ tsp.	2 mL
Freshly ground pepper, sprinkle		
Finely slivered fresh sweet basil	2 tbsp.	30 mL
Cornstarch	1 tsp.	5 mL
Skim evaporated milk	⅓ cup	75 mL

Cook pasta in boiling water and first amount of salt in large saucepan for 5 to 6 minutes, stirring occasionally, until tender but firm. Drain. Return to saucepan and keep warm.

Heat margarine in large non-stick skillet until bubbling. Stir in peach, tomato, brown sugar, salt and pepper. Cover. Cook for about 2 minutes until juices are released. Stir in basil.

Combine cornstarch and evaporated milk in small cup. Stir into peach mixture. Cook until bubbling. Pour skillet contents over pasta and toss together. Serves 3.

1 serving: 308 Calories; 2.5 g Total Fat (0.4 g Sat., 1.1 mg Cholesterol); 514 mg Sodium; 11 g Protein; 62 g Carbohydrate; 4 g Dietary Fiber

Pictured on page 35.

1. Easy Teriyaki Chicken Pasta, page 39
2. Thai Rice Noodles, page 62
3. Pasta Margarita, page 81
4. Pasta Paella, page 51
5. Peach Layered Dessert, page 46

Props Courtesy Of: Stokes
The Bay

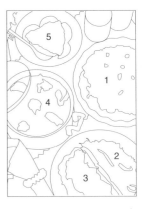

Baked Mozza Rigatoni

A great creamy cheese sauce you would never believe was low in fat!
Very quick and easy.

Skim milk	¹/₂ cup	125 mL
All-purpose flour	3 tbsp.	50 mL
Skim milk	1 cup	250 mL
Salt	¹/₂ tsp.	2 mL
Onion powder	¹/₄ tsp.	1 mL
Grated part-skim mozzarella cheese	1 cup	250 mL
Rigatoni (large tube pasta), 10 oz. (285 g)	4 cups	1 L
Boiling water	2¹/₂ qts.	2.5 L
Salt	2¹/₂ tsp.	12 mL
Paprika, sprinkle (optional)		

Combine first amount of milk and flour in small saucepan. Mix well until smooth. Add second amount of milk, first amount of salt and onion powder. Cook, stirring constantly, until boiling and slightly thickened.

Add cheese. Stir until melted.

Cook pasta in boiling water and second amount of salt in Dutch oven for about 11 minutes, stirring occasionally, until tender but firm. Drain. Turn into lightly greased 2 quart (2 L) shallow casserole dish. Pour sauce over top. Sprinkle with paprika. Cover. Bake in 375°F (190°C) oven for 15 minutes. Remove cover. Bake for 10 minutes until cheese is bubbling. Serves 4.

1 serving: 399 Calories; 6.3 g Total Fat (3.4 g Sat., 19.7 mg Cholesterol); 539 mg Sodium; 21 g Protein; 63 g Carbohydrate; 2 g Dietary Fiber

Pictured on page 72 and back cover.

1. Roasted Chicken And Vegetables, page 30
2. Spaghetti And Marinated Tomatoes, page 79
3. Baked Mozza Rigatoni, above
4. Spinach-Stuffed Cannelloni, page 139
5. Angel Hair Scampi, page 55
6. Easy Pasta Primavera, page 74

Props Courtesy Of: Chintz & Company
Eaton's
Stokes
The Basket House

Easy Pasta Primavera

Frozen vegetables make this a very easy and quick dish to prepare.

Frozen Italian-style vegetables	2¼ lbs.	1 kg
Water	¼ cup	60 mL
Diet tub margarine	2 tbsp.	30 mL
Dried sweet basil	¼ tsp.	1 mL
Dried whole oregano	¼ tsp.	1 mL
Frozen egg product, thawed	6 tbsp.	100 mL
Skim evaporated milk	½ cup	125 mL
Grated light Parmesan cheese product	¼ cup	60 mL
Spaghetti (string pasta)	10 oz.	285 g
Boiling water	3 qts.	3 L
Salt	1 tbsp.	15 mL
Ripe small plum tomatoes, diced	2-3	2-3
Finely chopped fresh parsley	1 tbsp.	15 mL

Place vegetables and water in 2 quart (2 L) microwave-safe casserole dish. Cover. Microwave on high (100%) for 6 minutes. Drain.

Melt margarine in large non-stick skillet. Add vegetables, basil and oregano. Cook for about 5 minutes, stirring often, until tender.

Beat egg product, evaporated milk and cheese together in small bowl.

Cook pasta in boiling water and salt in Dutch oven for 8 to 10 minutes, stirring occasionally, until tender but firm. Drain. Return to Dutch oven. Add milk mixture. Stir well.

Add vegetables, tomato and parsley. Toss until liquid is absorbed. Serves 4.

1 serving: 509 Calories; 5.7 g Total Fat (1.5 g Sat., 3.8 mg Cholesterol); 367 mg Sodium; 25 g Protein; 93 g Carbohydrate; 12 g Dietary Fiber

Pictured on page 72.

 Go easy when sprinkling on Parmesan cheese at the table. One tbsp. (15 mL) of grated fresh Parmesan cheese adds 2 grams of fat. Grated light Parmesan cheese product adds just under 1 gram of fat per 1 tbsp. (15 mL).

Spring "Butterflies"

Use fresh, young vegetables for best flavor and color. Be careful not to overcook.

Bow tie (medium) pasta (farfalle), 10 oz. (285 g)	4 cups	1 L
Boiling water	2½ qts.	2.5 L
Salt	2½ tsp.	12 mL
Garlic cloves, minced	4	4
Olive oil	1 tsp.	5 mL
Water	¼ cup	60 mL
White (or alcohol-free white) wine	¼ cup	60 mL
Julienned carrot, 2 inch (5 cm) pieces	1 cup	250 mL
Asparagus, tough ends removed and cut into 2 inch (5 cm) pieces	2 cups	500 mL
Red pepper, cut into 2 inch (5 cm) slivers	1	1
Fresh pea pods, trimmed (5 oz., 140 g)	2 cups	500 mL
Medium zucchini, with peel, cut julienne	1	1
Chopped ripe plum tomato	3 cups	750 mL
Basil Pesto, page 78 (or commercial)	1 tsp.	5 mL
Light spreadable cream cheese	3 tbsp.	50 mL
Grated light Parmesan cheese product	2 tbsp.	30 mL
Salt, sprinkle		
Freshly ground pepper, sprinkle		

Cook pasta in boiling water and salt in Dutch oven for 8 to 10 minutes until tender but firm. Drain and return to Dutch oven to stay warm.

Sauté garlic in oil in large non-stick skillet just until soft. Add water and wine. Bring to a boil. Add carrot. Cover. Cook for 1 minute. Add asparagus, red pepper and pea pods. Cover. Cook for 2 minutes. Add zucchini. Cook for 1 minute. Remove vegetables with slotted spoon to Dutch oven. Toss vegetables with pasta. Keep warm.

Cook tomato in remaining liquid in skillet for 4 to 5 minutes until soft and hot but still holding shape. Stir in pesto and cream cheese until mixture is bubbling. Pour over pasta and toss. Sprinkle with Parmesan cheese, salt and pepper. Serve immediately. Serves 6.

1 serving: 280 Calories; 4 g Total Fat (1.3 g Sat., 4.6 mg Cholesterol); 133 mg Sodium; 12 g Protein; 49 g Carbohydrate; 5 g Dietary Fiber

Pictured on page 35.

Yellow Pepper Pasta

This can be served as an accompaniment or first course.

YELLOW PEPPER SAUCE

Garlic cloves, minced	2	2
Olive oil	1 tbsp.	15 mL
Water	1/3 cup	75 mL
Vegetable bouillon powder	1 tsp.	5 mL
Dried crushed chilies, just a pinch		
Very finely chopped onion	1/2 cup	125 mL
Very finely chopped yellow pepper	2 cups	500 mL
Dried sweet basil	1 tsp.	5 mL
Salt	1/2 tsp.	2 mL
Chopped fresh parsley	2 tbsp.	30 mL
Vermicelli (thin string pasta)	8 oz.	225 g
Boiling water	2 qts.	2 L
Salt	2 tsp.	10 mL

Yellow Pepper Sauce: Sauté garlic in oil in large non-stick skillet until soft. Add water, bouillon powder and chilies. Bring to a boil.

Add onion, yellow pepper, basil and first amount of salt. Stir. Cover. Cook for 40 minutes, stirring occasionally, until onion and yellow pepper are very soft. Stir in parsley. Makes about 1 1/2 cups (375 mL) sauce.

Cook pasta in boiling water and second amount of salt in Dutch oven for 5 to 6 minutes, stirring occasionally, until tender but firm. Drain. Return to Dutch oven. Pour sauce over. Toss well. Serve immediately. Serves 4.

1 serving: 269 Calories; 4.6 g Total Fat (0.7 g Sat., 0.1 mg Cholesterol); 494 mg Sodium; 8 g Protein; 49 g Carbohydrate; 3 g Dietary Fiber

Pictured on page 90.

Lemon Stars

A great accompaniment to any meat. Try the many variations.

Lemon juice	1 tbsp.	15 mL
Condensed chicken broth	10 oz.	284 mL
Water	1 cup	250 mL
Vegetable bouillon powder	1 tsp.	5 mL
Uncooked star (very small) pasta (stelline)	1 cup	250 mL
Skim evaporated milk	1/2 cup	125 mL
Grated lemon peel	1/4 - 1/2 tsp.	1-2 mL

(continued on next page)

Combine first 4 ingredients in medium saucepan. Heat until boiling. Stir in pasta. Cover. Simmer for about 10 minutes until liquid is absorbed. Remove from heat.

Stir in evaporated milk and lemon peel. Serve immediately. Makes 2⅔ cups (650 mL).

¾ cup (175 mL): 322 Calories; 2.2 g Total Fat (0.5 g Sat., 2.3 mg Cholesterol); 750 mg Sodium; 16 g Protein; 58 g Carbohydrate; 2 g Dietary Fiber

Pictured on page 90.

Variation #1: Add 1 to 1½ tsp. (5 to 7 mL) dill weed to pasta with evaporated milk and lemon peel.

Variation #2: Add freshly ground pepper to taste.

Variation #3: Add ½ to 1 tsp. (2 to 5 mL) grated gingerroot with evaporated milk and lemon peel.

Variation #4: Add 2 tbsp. (30 mL) finely chopped green onion with evaporated milk and lemon peel.

Variation #5: Add 1 small minced garlic clove with liquid ingredients before bringing to a boil.

Cheese And Tomato Casserole

Only 15 minutes preparation time.

Elbow macaroni (small pasta), 8 oz. (225 g)	2 cups	500 mL
Boiling water	8 cups	2 L
Salt	2 tsp.	10 mL
Canned plum tomatoes, processed	14 oz.	398 mL
Onion powder	½ tsp.	2 mL
Dried sweet basil	1 tsp.	5 mL
Skim evaporated milk	½ cup	125 mL
All-purpose flour	1½ tbsp.	25 mL
Grated part-skim mozzarella cheese	1 cup	250 mL

Cook pasta in boiling water and salt in Dutch oven for 6 minutes, stirring occasionally, until tender but firm. Drain. Turn into greased 2 quart (2 L) shallow casserole dish.

Heat tomato, onion powder and basil in medium saucepan. Combine evaporated milk and flour in separate bowl. Mix until smooth. Add to tomato mixture. Heat until boiling and slightly thickened. Pour over pasta. Stir gently.

Sprinkle cheese over top. Cover. Bake in 375°F (190°C) oven for 20 minutes until hot and cheese is melted. Serves 4.

1 serving: 347 Calories; 6.1 g Total Fat (3.3 g Sat., 18.9 mg Cholesterol); 350 mg Sodium; 19 g Protein; 54 g Carbohydrate; 3 g Dietary Fiber

Fresh Garlic And Ginger Pasta

A pungent ginger aroma. Makes a great accompaniment to pork or chicken.

Spaghettini (thin string pasta)	10 oz.	285 g
Boiling water	3 qts.	3 L
Salt	1 tbsp.	15 mL
Garlic cloves, minced	2	2
Minced or grated gingerroot	1 tbsp.	15 mL
Dried crushed chilies, just a pinch		
Dried thyme	¼ tsp.	1 mL
Olive oil	1 tbsp.	15 mL
Sliced green onion	½ cup	125 mL
Condensed chicken broth (or 1 tsp., 5 mL, chicken bouillon powder, dissolved in ⅓ cup, 75 mL, warm water)	⅓ cup	75 mL
Freshly ground pepper, sprinkle		
Grated light Parmesan cheese product	2 tbsp.	30 mL

Cook pasta in boiling water and salt in Dutch oven for 8 to 10 minutes, stirring occasionally, until tender but firm. Drain. Return to Dutch oven.

Sauté garlic, ginger, chilies and thyme in oil in small skillet for about 2 minutes until garlic is soft. Add green onion. Sauté for 2 minutes. Add chicken broth and heat until hot. Pour over hot pasta.

Sprinkle with pepper and Parmesan cheese. Toss well. Serves 4.

1 serving: 319 Calories; 5.3 g Total Fat (1 g Sat., 1.5 mg Cholesterol); 201 mg Sodium; 12 g Protein; 55 g Carbohydrate; 2 g Dietary Fiber

Basil Pesto Linguine

Make double the amount of Basil Pesto and freeze in small quantities to flavor other sauces.

BASIL PESTO		
Olive oil	2 tbsp.	30 mL
Garlic clove, halved	1	1
Firmly packed fresh sweet basil	½ cup	125 mL
Grated light Parmesan cheese product	2 tbsp.	30 mL
White (or alcohol-free white) wine	4 tsp.	20 mL
Linguine (flat string pasta)	1 lb.	454 g
Boiling water	4 qts.	4 L
Salt	4 tsp.	20 mL

(continued on next page)

Meatless Dishes

Basil Pesto: Process first 5 ingredients in blender, scraping sides down occasionally, until mixture is thick and paste-like. Add 1 tsp. (5 mL) wine, if necessary, to help blend. Basil should be very finely chopped. Makes ¼ cup (60 mL) pesto.

Cook pasta in boiling water and salt in Dutch oven for 8 to 10 minutes, stirring occasionally, until tender but firm. Drain. Return to Dutch oven. Add pesto. Toss well. Serve immediately. Serves 6.

1 serving: 332 Calories; 6.1 g Total Fat (1 g Sat., 0.8 mg Cholesterol); 43 mg Sodium; 11 g Protein; 57 g Carbohydrate; 2 g Dietary Fiber

---

Spaghetti And Marinated Tomatoes

Marinated tomatoes can be stored for up to two days in the refrigerator. Bring to room temperature before combining with pasta. This dish can also be served warm by gently heating in microwave oven or saucepan.

Ripe medium plum tomatoes, finely diced	6	6
Olive oil	4 tsp.	20 mL
Large garlic clove, minced	1	1
Finely chopped fresh sweet basil leaves (or 2 tsp., 10 mL, dried)	2 tbsp.	30 mL
Tomato juice	¼ cup	60 mL
Lemon juice	2 tsp.	10 mL
Salt	½ tsp.	2 mL
Freshly ground pepper, sprinkle		
Spaghetti (string pasta)	10 oz.	285 g
Boiling water	3 qts.	3 L
Salt	1 tbsp.	15 mL
Grated light Parmesan cheese product, sprinkle (optional)		

Combine first 8 ingredients in medium bowl. Stir well. Cover. Let stand at room temperature for at least 1 hour to blend flavors.

Cook pasta in boiling water and second amount of salt in Dutch oven for 8 to 10 minutes, stirring occasionally, until tender but firm. Pour marinade over. Toss well.

Sprinkle with Parmesan cheese. Serves 4.

1 serving: 350 Calories; 6.3 g Total Fat (0.9 g Sat., 0 mg Cholesterol); 418 mg Sodium; 11 g Protein; 63 g Carbohydrate; 4 g Dietary Fiber

Pictured on page 72 and back cover.

Variation: Omit tomato juice and lemon juice and add ¼ cup (60 mL) white (or alcohol-free white) wine.

Gnocchi With Tomato Purée

It takes a bit of time to make the gnocchi but no time at all for the sauce.

Potato Gnocchi, page 84 (full recipe)	1½ lbs.	680 g
Water	4 qts.	4 L
Salt	1 tbsp.	15 mL
Garlic clove, minced	1	1
Olive oil	¼ tsp.	1 mL
Canned plum tomatoes, with juice, processed	14 oz.	398 mL
Granulated sugar, pinch		
Salt, sprinkle (optional)		
Freshly ground pepper, sprinkle		
Chopped fresh sweet basil (or 1 tsp., 5 mL, dried)	1 tbsp.	15 mL
Grated light Parmesan cheese product	2 tbsp.	30 mL
Grated part-skim mozzarella cheese (optional)	½ cup	125 mL

Simmer uncooked gnocchi, in 2 or 3 batches, in water and salt for about 6 minutes until they bob to the surface and remain on top for 1 minute. Remove with slotted spoon to lightly greased 2 quart (2 L) casserole dish.

Sauté garlic in oil in small non-stick skillet for about 30 seconds until soft. Add tomato, sugar, salt and pepper and boil for 5 minutes, uncovered, until slightly reduced.

Stir in basil. Makes 1½ cups (375 mL).

Pour tomato purée over gnocchi. Sprinkle with both cheeses. Bake, uncovered, in 350°F (175°C) oven for about 20 minutes. Serves 8.

1 serving: 240 Calories; 1 g Total Fat (0.3 g Sat., 0.6 mg Cholesterol); 115 mg Sodium; 7 g Protein; 51 g Carbohydrate; 3 g Dietary Fiber

Pictured on page 126.

 When cooking gnocchi, ensure that the water is gently simmering, not boiling rapidly. Rapidly boiling water can cause gnocchi to fall apart.

Pasta Margarita

This dish is the color of the Italian flag—red, green and white.

Linguine (flat string pasta)	8 oz.	225 g
Boiling water	2 qts.	2 L
Salt	2 tsp.	10 mL
Water	1/4 cup	60 mL
Vegetable bouillon powder	1/2 tsp.	2 mL
Garlic cloves, minced	2	2
Cornstarch	2 tsp.	10 mL
Water	1/4 cup	60 mL
Lightly packed fresh spinach leaves, stems removed	8 cups	2 L
Diced ripe plum tomato	3 cups	750 mL
Dried whole oregano	1/4-1/2 tsp.	1-2 mL
Salt, sprinkle		
Freshly ground pepper, sprinkle		
Pine nuts, toasted and chopped (optional)	2 tbsp.	30 mL

Cook linguine in boiling water and first amount of salt in Dutch oven for 8 to 10 minutes, stirring occasionally, until tender but firm. Drain. Keep warm.

Heat first amount of water and bouillon powder in large non-stick skillet. Sauté garlic for about 2 minutes until soft.

Combine cornstarch and second amount of water. Add to garlic mixture. Stir until boiling and thickened.

Stir in spinach. Cover. Cook for 2 to 3 minutes until just limp. Do not overcook. Add tomato and oregano. Stir gently. Cover. Cook for 3 minutes until tomato is warm.

Sprinkle with second amount of salt and pepper. Spoon over pasta. Toss. Sprinkle with pine nuts. Serves 4.

1 serving: 255 Calories; 1.5 g Total Fat (0.2 g Sat., trace Cholesterol); 144 mg Sodium; 10 g Protein; 51 g Carbohydrate; 5 g Dietary Fiber

Pictured on page 71.

 Toasting nuts before adding to a recipe will intensify their flavor; therefore, a little will go a long way.

Basil And Garlic Pasta Dough

Very tasty.

All-purpose flour (or durum semolina)	2 cups	500 mL
Salt	1 tsp.	5 mL
Garlic cloves, minced	5	5
Dried sweet basil, crushed	1 tsp.	5 mL
Frozen egg product, thawed	⅓ cup	75 mL
Warm water, approximately	⅓ cup	75 mL

Combine flour, salt, garlic and basil in food processor or large bowl.

Combine egg product and warm water in small cup. Gradually add through tube of food processor, while processing, until mixture forms ball. Or gradually mix into flour mixture in bowl until soft ball forms. Add bit more water if dough is too dry. Knead on lightly floured surface until smooth. Cover with plastic wrap. Let rest for 30 minutes.

Roll out ¼ of dough very thin (about ¹⁄₁₆ inch, 1.5 mm) on lightly floured surface, dusting with all-purpose flour as needed to prevent sticking. Let stand for 10 minutes to dry. Flip over. Let stand for 10 minutes. Roll up loosely, like jelly roll. To make noodles, use sharp knife and cut crosswise into ¼ inch (6 mm) slices. Toss gently to unroll. Repeat until all dough is used. Makes about 1 lb. (454 g) uncooked pasta.

3 oz. (85 g) uncooked pasta: 193 Calories; 0.6 g Total Fat (0.1 g Sat., 0 mg Cholesterol); 540 mg Sodium; 7 g Protein; 39 g Carbohydrate; 2 g Dietary Fiber

Chili Pepper Pasta Dough

A subtle hint of "heat."

All-purpose flour (or durum semolina)	2 cups	500 mL
Salt	1 tsp.	5 mL
Finely crushed dried crushed chilies	2 tsp.	10 mL
Frozen egg product, thawed	⅓ cup	75 mL
Tomato juice (or water), approximately	⅓ cup	75 mL

Combine flour, salt and chilies in food processor or large bowl.

Combine egg product and tomato juice in small cup. Gradually add through tube of food processor, while processing, until mixture forms ball. Or gradually mix into flour mixture in bowl until soft ball forms. Add bit more tomato juice if dough is too dry. Knead on lightly floured surface until smooth. Cover with plastic wrap. Let rest for 30 minutes.

(continued on next page)

Roll out ½ of dough very thin (about ¹⁄₁₆ inch, 1.5 mm) on lightly floured surface, dusting with all-purpose flour as needed to prevent sticking. Let stand for 10 minutes to dry. Flip over. Let stand for 10 minutes. Roll up loosely, like jelly roll. To make noodles, use sharp knife and cut crosswise into ¼ inch (6 mm) slices. Toss gently to unroll. Repeat with remaining ½ of dough. Makes 1 lb. (454 g) uncooked pasta.

3 oz. (85 g) uncooked pasta: 193 Calories; 0.7 g Total Fat (0.1 g Sat., 0 mg Cholesterol); 596 mg Sodium; 7 g Protein; 39 g Carbohydrate; 2 g Dietary Fiber

Pictured on page 108.

Green Onion Pasta Dough

A white dough with bits of green onion for color.

Green onions, chopped	3	3
Frozen egg product, thawed	⅓ cup	75 mL
Warm water, approximately	⅔ cup	150 mL
All-purpose flour	2½ cups	625 mL
Salt	1 tsp.	5 mL

Combine green onion, egg product and warm water in blender. Process until onion is very finely minced.

Combine flour and salt in food processor or large bowl. Gradually add onion mixture through tube of processor, while processing, until mixture forms ball. Or gradually mix into flour mixture in bowl until soft ball forms. Add bit more water if dough is too dry. Knead on lightly floured surface until smooth. Cover with plastic wrap. Let rest for 30 minutes.

Roll out ½ of dough very thin (about ¹⁄₁₆ inch, 1.5 mm) on lightly floured surface, dusting with flour as needed to prevent sticking. Let stand for 10 minutes to dry. Flip over. Let stand for 10 minutes. Roll up loosely, like jelly roll. To make noodles, use sharp knife and cut crosswise into ¼ inch (6 mm) slices. Toss to unroll. Repeat until all dough is used. Makes 1¼ lbs. (560 g) uncooked pasta.

3 oz. (85 g) uncooked pasta: 187 Calories; 0.6 g Total Fat (0.1 g Sat., 0 mg Cholesterol); 432 mg Sodium; 7 g Protein; 38 g Carbohydrate; 2 g Dietary Fiber

Pictured on page 108.

tip   *Making fresh pasta dough in your food processor is very easy because the food processor kneads the dough for you. Once the dough forms a ball, let it process for another minute.*

Potato Gnocchi

Gnocchi (NYOH-kee) is Italian for "dumplings." Delicious served with Easy Spicy Tomato Sauce, page 110, Basil Pesto, page 78, or Bolognese Sauce, page 114.

Potatoes, peeled (about 6 medium)	1½ lbs.	680 g
Water	2 cups	500 mL
Salt	2 tsp.	10 mL
All-purpose flour, approximately	2½ cups	625 mL

Cut potatoes into uniform-sized pieces. Place in medium saucepan with water and salt. Bring to a boil. Cook potatoes until soft. Drain off water. Sieve hot potatoes into large bowl. Gradually stir in enough flour until stiff dough is formed. (Amount of flour will be determined by water content of potatoes.)

Roll pieces of dough into ropes, ½ to ¾ inch (12 to 20 mm) in diameter, on lightly floured surface. Cut ropes into 1 inch (2.5 cm) lengths. Each gnocchi can be patterned by gently rolling down rough side of grater. Makes 8 cups (2 L).

1 cup (250 mL): 223 Calories; 0.5 g Total Fat (0.1 g Sat., trace Cholesterol); 5 mg Sodium; 6 g Protein; 49 g Carbohydrate; 2 g Dietary Fiber

Lemon Pepper Pasta Dough

Great with seafood, wine sauces or in Creamed Broccoli Soup, page 122.

All-purpose flour	2½ cups	625 mL
Salt	1 tsp.	5 mL
Grated peel of 1 lemon		
Freshly ground pepper	1 tsp.	5 mL
Juice of 1 lemon, plus water to make	⅔ cup	150 mL
Frozen egg product, thawed	⅓ cup	75 mL

Combine flour, salt, lemon peel and pepper in food processor or large bowl.

Combine lemon juice, water and egg product in small cup. Gradually add through tube of food processor, while processing, until mixture forms ball. Or gradually mix into flour mixture in bowl and mix until soft ball forms. Add bit more water if dough is too dry. Turn out onto lightly floured surface. Knead until smooth. Cover with plastic wrap. Let rest for 30 minutes.

Roll out ½ of dough very thin (about 1⁄16 inch, 1.5 mm) on lightly floured surface, dusting with flour as needed to prevent sticking. Let stand for 10 minutes to dry. Flip over. Let stand for 10 minutes. Roll up loosely, like jelly roll. To make noodles, use sharp knife and cut crosswise into ¼ inch (6 mm) slices. Toss gently to unroll. Repeat until all dough is used. Makes 1¼ lbs. (560 g) uncooked pasta.

3 oz. (85 g) uncooked pasta: 191 Calories; 0.6 g Total Fat (0.1 g Sat., 0 mg Cholesterol); 432 mg Sodium; 7 g Protein; 40 g Carbohydrate; 2 g Dietary Fiber

Whole Wheat Pasta Dough

Very tender.

Whole wheat flour	2¼ cups	560 mL
Salt	1 tsp.	5 mL
Warm water, approximately	½ cup	125 mL
Frozen egg product, thawed	6 tbsp.	100 mL
Olive oil	1 tsp.	5 mL

Combine flour and salt in food processor or large bowl.

Combine warm water, egg product and oil in small cup. Gradually add through tube of food processor, while processing, until mixture forms ball. Or gradually mix into flour mixture in bowl until soft ball forms. Add bit more water if dough is too dry. Knead on lightly floured surface until smooth. Form into ball. Cover with plastic wrap. Let rest for 30 minutes.

Roll out ¼ of dough very thin (about ¹⁄₁₆ inch, 1.5 mm) on lightly floured surface, dusting with flour as needed to prevent sticking. Let stand for 10 minutes to dry. Flip over. Let stand for 10 minutes. Roll up loosely, like jelly roll. To make noodles, use sharp knife and cut crosswise into ¼ inch (6 mm) slices. Toss gently to unroll. Repeat with remaining ½ of dough. Makes about 1 lb. (454 g) uncooked pasta.

3 oz. (85 g) uncooked pasta: *198 Calories; 2 g Total Fat (0.3 g Sat., 0 mg Cholesterol); 544 mg Sodium; 9 g Protein; 39 g Carbohydrate; 7 g Dietary Fiber*

Pictured on page 108.

Paré Pointer
A ghost's favorite cereal is covered with evaporated milk.

Basic Pasta Dough

Durum semolina can be found at most large grocery or specialty stores.

All-purpose flour (or durum semolina), approximately	3 cups	750 mL
Salt	1 tsp.	5 mL
Warm water, approximately	1 cup	250 mL

Place flour and salt in food processor or large bowl. Make a well in center.

Gradually add warm water through tube of food processor, while processing, until mixture forms ball. Or gradually mix into flour mixture in bowl until soft ball forms. Add bit more water if dough is too dry. Knead until smooth. Cover with plastic wrap. Let rest for 15 minutes.

Roll out ¼ of dough very thin (about ¹/₁₆ inch, 1.5 mm) on lightly floured surface, dusting with all-purpose flour as needed to prevent sticking. Let stand for 10 minutes to dry. Flip over. Let stand for 10 minutes. Roll up loosely, like jelly roll. To make noodles, use sharp knife and cut crosswise into ¼ inch (6 mm) slices. Toss gently to unroll. Sprinkle with bit of all-purpose flour to prevent sticking. Toss. Repeat until all dough is used. Makes about 1½ lbs. (680 g) uncooked pasta.

3 oz. (85 g) uncooked pasta: 180 Calories; 0.5 g Total Fat (0.1 g Sat., 0 mg Cholesterol); 340 mg Sodium; 5 g Protein; 38 g Carbohydrate; 2 g Dietary Fiber

LASAGNE NOODLES: After rolling out to about ¹/₁₆ inch (1.5 mm) thickness, cut into 2 x 10 inch (5 x 25 cm) strips, for lasagne.

SOUP NOODLES: Roll out ¼ of dough very thin (about ¹/₁₆ inch, 1.5 mm) on lightly floured surface, dusting with all-purpose flour as needed to prevent sticking. Cut into long 4 inch (10 cm) wide strips. Let stand on lightly floured surface for 10 minutes to dry. Flip over. Dry for 10 minutes. Stack strips on top of one another. Cut with sharp knife angled one way and then the other to create irregularly shaped, short noodles.

 Whole wheat pasta takes longer to reach the al dente stage than a pasta made with all-purpose flour. Whole wheat pasta has a delicious nutty flavor and color. Top with colorful, seasoned sauces rather than pale, creamy ones.

Egg Pasta Dough

This egg product makes this a low-fat pasta.

All-purpose flour (or durum semolina)	3 cups	750 mL
Salt	1 tsp.	5 mL
Frozen egg product, thawed	8 oz.	227 mL
Warm Water	1-2 tbsp.	15-30 mL

Place flour and salt in food processor or large bowl. Make a well in center.

Gradually add egg product and warm water through a tube of food processor, while processing, until mixture forms ball. Or gradually mix into flour mixture in bowl until soft ball forms. Add a bit more water if dough is too dry. Knead until smooth. Cover with plastic wrap. Let rest for 30 minutes.

Roll out ¼ of dough very thin (about ¹⁄₁₆ inch, 1.5 mm) on lightly floured surface, dusting with all-purpose flour as needed to prevent sticking. Let stand for 10 minutes to dry. Flip over. Let stand for 10 minutes. Roll up loosely, like jelly roll. To make noodles, use sharp knife and cut crosswise into ¼ inch (6 mm) slices. toss gently to unroll. Sprinkle with bit of all-purpose flour to prevent sticking. Toss. Repeat until all dough is used. Makes about 1½ lbs. (680 g) uncooked pasta.

3 oz. (85 g) uncooked pasta: 196 Calories; 0.7 g Total Fat (0.1 g Sat., 0 mg Cholesterol); 395 mg Sodium; 8 g Protein; 38 g Catbohydrate; 2 g Dietary Fiber

 If cooked pasta has been left sitting too long and has stuck together, place in larger container and pour hot (not boiling) water over. Or, save some of the pasta water; it can be used for the same purpose. Quickly stir to break up pasta. Drain and use immediately.

Ham And Noodle Bake

A rich, mellow sauce. Only 15 minutes preparation time.

Large yolk-free broad noodles (8 oz., 225 g)	4 cups	1 L
Boiling water	2 qts.	2 L
Salt	2 tsp.	10 mL
Medium onion, finely chopped	½	½
Tub margarine	2 tsp.	10 mL
Chopped lean ham	4 oz.	113 g
Non-fat cottage cheese	⅔ cup	150 mL
Frozen egg product, thawed	⅓ cup	75 mL
Light spreadable cream cheese	¼ cup	60 mL
Salt	½ tsp.	2 mL
Pepper	⅛ tsp.	0.5 mL
Medium tomatoes, sliced	2	2
Paprika, sprinkle		

Cook noodles in boiling water and first amount of salt in large saucepan for about 10 minutes, stirring occasionally, until tender but firm. Drain. Rinse with cold water. Drain. Place noodles in greased 2 quart (2 L) casserole dish.

Sauté onion in margarine in small non-stick skillet until soft. Add to noodles. Stir in ham.

Combine next 5 ingredients in blender. Process until smooth. Add to noodle mixture. Mix well.

Arrange tomato over noodles, overlapping if necessary.

Sprinkle with paprika. Bake, uncovered, in 325°F (160°C) oven for about 30 minutes until firm. Serves 6.

1 serving: 195 Calories; 4 g Total Fat (1.5 g Sat., 14.1 mg Cholesterol); 693 mg Sodium; 15 g Protein; 25 g Carbohydrate; 1 g Dietary Fiber

Pictured on page 18.

1. Hunan Chicken Sauce, page 106
2. Coconut Curry Sauce, page 105
3. Oriental Beef And Vegetables, page 23
4. Asian Fish Fry, page 58
5. Lentil And Pasta Soup, page 120
6. Indonesian Dinner, page 92

Props Courtesy Of: Chintz & Company
Stokes
The Basket House

Pork Dishes

Pasta Alla Carbonara

The creamy sauce makes this dish a "comfort meal." Serve with buns and a salad.

White (or alcohol-free white) wine	½ cup	125 mL
Lean back bacon, finely diced	3 oz.	85 g
Garlic clove, minced	1	1
Medium shallot, finely chopped	1	1
Skim evaporated milk	13½ oz.	385 mL
Frozen egg product, thawed	8 oz.	227 mL
Grated light Parmesan cheese product	2 tbsp.	30 mL
Salt	½ tsp.	2 mL
Spaghetti (string pasta)	8 oz.	225 g
Boiling water	2 qts.	2 L
Salt	2 tsp.	10 mL
Cooked tiny peas	1 cup	250 mL

Freshly ground pepper, sprinkle

Simmer wine in medium saucepan. Add back bacon, garlic and shallot. Simmer, stirring occasionally, until shallot is soft.

Combine evaporated milk, egg product, Parmesan cheese and first amount of salt in bowl. Whisk into wine mixture. Cook for 5 to 6 minutes, whisking constantly.

Cook spaghetti in boiling water and second amount of salt in Dutch oven for 8 to 10 minutes, stirring occasionally, until tender. Drain. Return to Dutch oven. Pour sauce over. Add peas. Toss lightly. Cover. Let stand for 5 to 10 minutes. Toss.

Sprinkle pepper over top. Serves 4.

1 serving: 425 Calories; 3.5 g Total Fat (1.1 g Sat., 15.6 mg Cholesterol); 932 mg Sodium; 30 g Protein; 63 g Carbohydrate; 4 g Dietary Fiber

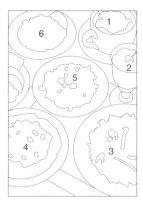

1. Herbed Tomato Soup, page 118
2. Ambrosia Dessert, page 47
3. Ginger Chicken Salad, page 102
4. Yellow Pepper Pasta, page 76
5. Cold Mushroom Salsa, page 113
6. Lemon Stars, page 76

Props Courtesy Of: The Bay

Indonesian Dinner

Only about ten minutes preparation time. Not too spicy.

Vermicelli (thin string pasta), broken in half	8 oz.	225 g
Boiling water	2 qts.	2 L
Salt	2 tsp.	10 mL
Boneless pork loin, trimmed of fat, diced into ½ inch (12 mm) pieces	½ lb.	225 g
Large onion, chopped	1	1
Garlic cloves, minced	3	3
Cooking oil	2 tsp.	10 mL
Oyster sauce	3 tbsp.	50 mL
Chili powder	2 tsp.	10 mL
Curry paste (available in ethnic section of grocery stores)	1 tsp.	5 mL
Thinly sliced celery, cut on the diagonal	2 cups	500 mL
Small cabbage, thinly shredded	½	½
Low-sodium soy sauce	3 tbsp.	50 mL
Salt	½ tsp.	2 mL
Pepper, sprinkle		
Cooked shrimp	6 oz.	170 g

Cook pasta in boiling water and first amount of salt in Dutch oven for 5 to 6 minutes, stirring occasionally, until tender but firm. Drain. Rinse with cold water. Drain.

Sauté pork, onion and garlic in oil in large non-stick wok for about 5 minutes.

Stir in next 8 ingredients. Cover. Cook for 6 minutes until cabbage is cooked and reduced in size.

Add pasta and shrimp. Stir until hot. Serve immediately. Serves 8.

1 serving: 220 Calories; 3.9 g Total Fat (0.8 g Sat., 57.9 mg Cholesterol); 632 mg Sodium; 16 g Protein; 30 g Carbohydrate; 2 g Dietary Fiber

Pictured on page 89.

Pork Dishes

Basil Cream Fiesta

A cool, refreshing salad on a warm summer day.

Tri-colored fusilli (spiral pasta), 8 oz. (225 g)	2⅔ cups	650 mL
Boiling water	3 qts.	3 L
Salt	1 tbsp.	15 mL
Broccoli florets	2 cups	500 mL
Cauliflower florets	2 cups	500 mL
Thinly sliced carrot	1 cup	250 mL
Diced green pepper	½ cup	125 mL
Diced red or yellow pepper	½ cup	125 mL
Green onions, sliced	2	2
Non-fat plain yogurt	½ cup	125 mL
Non-fat sour cream	½ cup	125 mL
White (or alcohol-free white) wine	¼ cup	60 mL
Basil Pesto, page 78 (or commercial)	1 tbsp.	15 mL
Garlic clove, minced	1	1
Dry mustard	½ tsp.	2 mL
Dried whole oregano, crushed	½ tsp.	2 mL
Salt	1 tsp.	5 mL
Freshly ground pepper, sprinkle		
Halved cherry tomatoes (or diced tomato)	1 cup	250 mL

Cook pasta in boiling water and first amount of salt in Dutch oven for about 7 minutes, stirring occasionally. Pasta should be slightly firm.

Add broccoli, cauliflower and carrot. Bring to a boil. Boil for 1 minute. Drain. Rinse with cold water. Drain. Place in large bowl.

Add peppers and green onion. Toss.

Combine next 9 ingredients in small bowl. Mix until smooth. Add to pasta mixture. Stir gently to coat. Cover and chill.

Place tomato halves over individual servings. Makes 10 cups (2.5 L).

1 cup (250 mL): 129 Calories; 1.4 g Total Fat (0.2 g Sat., 0.4 mg Cholesterol); 308 mg Sodium; 5 g Protein; 23 g Carbohydrate; 2 g Dietary Fiber

Pictured on page 17.

 Small and medium pastas (see pages 11 and 12) such as penne, shell, macaroni and fusilli are commonly used for salads. For a change, try a string pasta (round or flat) such as vermicelli, linguine or angel hair pasta. They can be left long, or broken in half or thirds.

Tortellini And Tzatziki Salad

Tzatziki (tsah-TSEE-kee) dressing gives this pasta salad
a Greek touch. Serve pita bread on the side.

TZATZIKI DRESSING		
Grated English cucumber, with peel	1 cup	250 mL
Salt	1 tsp.	5 mL
Non-fat plain yogurt	1 cup	250 mL
Garlic clove, minced	1	1
Chopped fresh mint	2 tbsp.	30 mL
Liquid honey	1 tsp.	5 mL
Salt	1/8 tsp.	0.5 mL
SALAD		
Fresh (or frozen or dried) cheese-filled tortellini (2 cups, 500 mL)	1/2 lb.	225 g
Boiling water	2 qts.	2 L
Salt	2 tsp.	10 mL
Small red onion, thinly sliced	1	1
Medium celery rib, thinly sliced	1	1
Green, red, orange or yellow pepper, thinly slivered	1/2	1/2
Cherry tomatoes, halved (or 1 medium tomato, seeded and diced)	10	10

Tzatziki Dressing: Place cucumber in colander over medium bowl. Sprinkle with first amount of salt. Stir. Let cucumber drain for 30 minutes, pressing several times to squeeze out as much liquid as possible. Place in medium bowl. Add yogurt, garlic, mint, honey and second amount of salt. Mix well. Chill for at least 2 hours. Makes 1 2/3 cups (400 mL) dressing.

Salad: Cook pasta in boiling water and third amount of salt in Dutch oven for 10 to 12 minutes, stirring occasionally, until tender but firm. Drain. Rinse with cold water. Drain. Place in large bowl.

Add onion, celery, green pepper and tomato. Stir. Cover and chill. Toss with dressing just before serving. Makes 7 cups (1.75 L).

1 cup (250 mL): 102 Calories; 2.9 g Total Fat (trace Sat., 20 mg Cholesterol); 554 mg Sodium; 6 g Protein; 13 g Carbohydrate; 1 g Dietary Fiber

Pictured on page 107.

Creamy Shrimp Salad

Serve this salad in butter lettuce cups or hollowed-out tomato halves.
Can also be served on a bed of crisp lettuce.

Tiny shell (very small) pasta	1 cup	250 mL
Boiling water	6 cups	1.5 L
Salt	1½ tsp.	7 mL
Medium ripe tomatoes, seeded and diced	3	3
Finely diced green pepper	½ cup	125 mL
Fresh or frozen cooked small shrimp (5½ oz., 154 g)	1 cup	250 mL
Green onions, thinly sliced	2	2
Non-fat salad dressing (or mayonnaise)	¼ cup	60 mL
Non-fat sour cream	¼ cup	60 mL
Seafood cocktail sauce	3 tbsp.	50 mL
Lemon juice	1 tbsp.	15 mL
Prepared horseradish	¼ tsp.	1 mL
Granulated sugar	⅛ tsp.	0.5 mL
Salt	⅛ tsp.	0.5 mL
Freshly ground pepper, sprinkle		

Cook pasta in boiling water and first amount of salt in large saucepan for 10 to 12 minutes, stirring occasionally, until tender but firm. Drain. Rinse with cold water. Drain. Place in medium bowl.

Add tomato, green pepper, shrimp and green onion. Toss.

Mix remaining 8 ingredients in small bowl. Pour over pasta mixture. Mix well. Makes 6 cups (1.5 L).

1 cup (250 mL): 125 Calories; 0.8 g Total Fat (0.1 g Sat., 44 mg Cholesterol); 294 mg Sodium; 8 g Protein; 21 g Carbohydrate; 1 g Dietary Fiber

Pictured on page 35.

 Make a thin sauce using orange juice or tomato juice, plus vinegar and herbs to taste. Heat and thicken with 1 tsp. (5 mL) cornstarch for 1 cup (250 mL). Chill. This makes a good substitute for vinaigrette dressings in salads.

Pasta Bean Salad

The perfect salad to take on a picnic.

BALSAMIC DRESSING

Non-fat Italian dressing	1/2 cup	125 mL
Reserved juice from tomatoes		
Grated light Parmesan cheese product	2 tbsp.	30 mL
Balsamic vinegar	1 tbsp.	15 mL
Small garlic clove, minced	1	1
Granulated sugar	1 tsp.	5 mL
Dried sweet basil, just a pinch		
Dried thyme, just a pinch		

SALAD

Elbow macaroni (small pasta), 8 oz. (225 g)	2 cups	500 mL
Boiling water	2 qts.	2 L
Salt	2 tsp.	10 mL
Canned mixed beans, drained and rinsed	19 oz.	540 mL
Medium red onion, thinly sliced	1/2	1/2
Green, red, orange or yellow pepper, thinly sliced into 2 inch (5 cm) lengths	1/2	1/2
Medium carrot, coarsely grated	1	1
Canned stewed tomatoes, drained, chopped and juice reserved	14 oz.	398 mL

Balsamic Dressing: Combine all 8 ingredients in jar. Cover. Shake well. Let stand for 15 minutes to blend flavors. Makes 1 1/3 cups (325 mL) dressing.

Salad: Cook pasta in boiling water and salt in large saucepan for about 8 minutes, stirring occasionally, until tender but firm. Do not overcook. Drain. Rinse with cold water. Drain. Place in large bowl.

Add remaining 5 ingredients to pasta. Pour dressing over. Mix well. May be served immediately or covered and refrigerated to serve cold. Makes 8 cups (2 L).

1 cup (250 mL): 178 Calories; 1.1 g Total Fat (0.3 g Sat., 0.6 mg Cholesterol); 421 mg Sodium; 7 g Protein; 35 g Carbohydrate; 4 g Dietary Fiber

Pictured on page 107.

Little Stuffed Tomatoes

Firm and fleshy plum tomatoes make great "shells" to contain filling.

Small firm plum tomatoes	8	8
Salt	½ tsp.	2 mL
Tiny bow tie (very small) pasta	⅔ cup	150 mL
Boiling water	4 cups	1 L
Salt	1 tsp.	5 mL
Non-fat spreadable herb & garlic-flavored cream cheese	¼ cup	60 mL
Non-fat sour cream	¼ cup	60 mL
Finely chopped English cucumber, with peel	½ cup	125 mL
Finely chopped green onion	1 tbsp.	15 mL
Finely chopped fresh sweet basil	2 tsp.	10 mL
Chopped fresh parsley	2 tsp.	10 mL
Salt	½ tsp.	2 mL
Freshly ground pepper, sprinkle		

Cut tomatoes in half lengthwise. Scoop out inner pulp, discarding juice and seeds. Measure ½ cup (125 mL) pulp, discarding any extra. Sprinkle insides of tomatoes with first amount of salt. Turn upside down on paper towel. Let stand for 30 minutes to drain. Blot insides of tomato halves with paper towel to dry well.

Cook pasta in boiling water and second amount of salt in medium saucepan for 6 to 7 minutes, stirring occasionally, until tender but firm. Drain. Rinse with cold water. Drain.

Combine cream cheese and sour cream in medium bowl. Mix until smooth.

Stir in pasta. Add reserved tomato flesh, cucumber, green onion, basil, parsley, third amount of salt and pepper. Mix well. Cover. Chill until tomatoes are ready to be filled. Spoon a rounded tablespoonful of filling into each tomato half. Makes 16.

1 filled tomato half: 32 Calories; 0.3 g Total Fat (trace Sat., 0 mg Cholesterol); 177 mg Sodium; 1 g Protein; 7 g Carbohydrate; 1 g Dietary Fiber

Pictured on page 17.

 Plum tomatoes, whether fresh or canned, are the best for making tomato-based sauces. This flavorful egg-shaped tomato goes nicely with the blander flavor of pasta.

Stuffed Tomato Salad

A genuine summer salad when you use vine-ripened tomatoes.

Medium tomatoes, hollowed out and inside flesh reserved	6	6
Salt	1 tsp.	5 mL
Orzo (very small pasta)	½ cup	125 mL
Boiling water	4 cups	1 L
Salt	1 tsp.	5 mL
White (or alcohol-free white) wine	¼ cup	60 mL
Balsamic vinegar	1 tsp.	5 mL
Reserved tomato flesh, chopped (remove some seeds if desired)	1 cup	250 mL
Basil Pesto, page 78 (or commercial)	1 tsp.	5 mL
Pectin granules	½ tsp.	2 mL
Freshly ground pepper, sprinkle		
Green onion, sliced	1	1
Diced green, red, orange or yellow pepper	¼ cup	60 mL
Thinly shredded radicchio	¼ cup	60 mL
Grated carrot	¼ cup	60 mL

Sprinkle insides of tomatoes with first amount of salt. Turn upside down on paper towel to drain well.

Cook pasta in boiling water and second amount of salt in large saucepan for 8 to 10 minutes, stirring occasionally, until tender but firm. Drain. Rinse with cold water. Drain. Place in medium bowl.

Combine next 6 ingredients in sealable jar or container. Cover and shake well to mix. Pour over pasta.

Stir in remaining 4 ingredients. Toss well. Stuff each tomato with salad. Makes 6 stuffed tomatoes.

1 stuffed tomato: 119 Calories; 1.3 g Total Fat (0.2 g Sat., 0.1 mg Cholesterol); 471 mg Sodium; 4 g Protein; 22 g Carbohydrate; 2 g Dietary Fiber

Pictured on the front cover.

 Instead of just slicing vegetables, cut diagonally or julienne. Use a regular peeler for thin flat strips or a zester to get long thin "strings," or grate for a "light" salad or quick cooking sauce.

Oriental Pasta Salad

Very easy to assemble. Only 15 minutes preparation time.
Enjoy this pasta salad—Oriental style.

Vermicelli (thin string pasta)	6 oz.	170 g
Boiling water	6 cups	1.5 L
Salt	1½ tsp.	7 mL
Very thinly sliced green or purple cabbage	3 cups	750 mL
Canned sliced water chestnuts, drained	8 oz.	227 mL
Celery rib, thinly sliced on the diagonal	1	1
Red or yellow pepper, thinly sliced into 2 inch (5 cm) lengths	1	1
Thinly sliced fresh mushrooms	1 cup	250 mL
Green onions, thinly sliced	2	2
ORIENTAL DRESSING		
Rice vinegar	3 tbsp.	50 mL
Sherry (or alcohol-free sherry)	1 tbsp.	15 mL
Low-sodium soy sauce	1 tbsp.	15 mL
Hoisin sauce	1 tbsp.	15 mL
Granulated sugar	1 tsp.	5 mL
Sesame seed oil	2 tsp.	10 mL
Toasted sesame seed	2 tsp.	10 mL

Cook pasta in boiling water and salt in large saucepan for 5 to 6 minutes, stirring occasionally, until tender but firm. Drain. Rinse with cold water. Drain. Place in large bowl.

Add next 6 ingredients. Mix.

Oriental Dressing: Combine all 7 ingredients in small bowl. Whisk together. Makes about ½ cup (125 mL) dressing. Pour over salad. Toss well. May be served immediately or covered and refrigerated to serve cold. Makes 10 cups (2.5 L).

1 cup (250 mL): 103 Calories; 1.6 g Total Fat (0.2 g Sat., 0 mg Cholesterol); 146 mg Sodium; 3 g Protein; 19 g Carbohydrate; 2 g Dietary Fiber

Pictured on page 17.

 Dried pasta seldom contains eggs, but fresh pasta is often made with eggs instead of water. Be sure to read labels carefully, and if you have an allergy to eggs, ask restaurants about their pasta when dining out.

Fruity Turkey Salad

Use up your leftover turkey in this. A delicate curry flavor.
Enjoy as a main course or side salad.

CREAMY FRUIT DRESSING		
Non-fat ranch dressing	½ cup	125 mL
Non-fat plain yogurt (or light sour cream)	¼ cup	60 mL
Reserved fruit cocktail juice	2 tbsp.	30 mL
Curry powder	1 tsp.	5 mL
SALAD		
Bow tie (medium) pasta (farfalle), 6 oz. (170 g)	2½ cups	625 mL
Boiling water	2 qts.	2 L
Salt	2 tsp.	10 mL
Frozen peas	1 cup	250 mL
Diced cooked turkey breast, cut into ½ inch (12 mm) cubes	1½ cups	375 mL
Celery rib, thinly sliced	1	1
Green onion, thinly sliced	1	1
Diced pimiento (or roasted red pepper), optional	¼ cup	60 mL
Canned fruit cocktail, drained and juice reserved	14 oz.	398 mL

Creamy Fruit Dressing: Combine all 4 ingredients in small cup. Let stand for 15 minutes to blend flavors. Makes ¾ cup (175 mL) dressing.

Salad: Cook pasta in boiling water and salt in large saucepan for 10 minutes, stirring occasionally. Pasta should be undercooked. Add peas. Boil for 1 minute. Drain. Rinse with cold water. Drain. Place in medium bowl.

Add remaining 5 ingredients. Pour dressing over. Toss well. Chill for at least 1 hour before serving. Makes 7 cups (1.75 L).

1 cup (250 mL): 214 Calories; 0.8 g Total Fat (0.2 g Sat., 26.9 mg Cholesterol); 242 mg Sodium; 15 g Protein; 36 g Carbohydrate; 3 g Dietary Fiber

Pictured on page 107.

 Make commercial non-fat or low-fat salad dressing taste even better by adding herbs, flavored vinegar or mustard.

Cool Sweet 'N' Sour Pasta

This salad can be made ahead of time. Keeps well in the refrigerator for up to three days.

Thinly sliced carrot	3 cups	750 mL
Boiling water	1 cup	250 mL
Salt, just a pinch		
Garlic cloves, minced	2	2
Cooking oil	2 tsp.	10 mL
Tomato sauce	7½ oz.	213 mL
Granulated sugar	½ cup	125 mL
White vinegar	½ cup	125 mL
Prepared mustard	2 tsp.	10 mL
Thinly sliced onion	1 cup	250 mL
Slivered red or green pepper	1 cup	250 mL
Fusilli (spiral pasta), 7 oz. (200 g)	2 cups	500 mL
Boiling water	2 qts.	2 L
Salt	2 tsp.	10 mL
Diced English cucumber, with peel	1 cup	250 mL

Cook carrot in boiling water and salt in medium saucepan for about 8 minutes until tender-crisp. Drain.

Sauté garlic in oil in large saucepan until soft but not brown. Stir in tomato sauce, sugar, vinegar and mustard. Bring to a boil. Stir in onion and green pepper. Cook, uncovered, for 1 minute. Remove from heat. Place in medium bowl. Add carrot. Stir. Cover and chill.

Cook pasta in boiling water and salt in large saucepan for 8 minutes, stirring occasionally, until tender but firm. Drain. Rinse with cold water. Drain. Place in large bowl.

Add carrot mixture. Add cucumber. Mix well. Makes 8 cups (2 L).

1 cup (250 mL): 198 Calories; 1.8 g Total Fat (0.2 g Sat., 0 mg Cholesterol); 204 mg Sodium; 5 g Protein; 42 g Carbohydrate; 3 g Dietary Fiber

Pictured on page 17.

 Dressings made with pectin granules will cling better to salad ingredients and not just seep to the bottom of the bowl.

Ginger Chicken Salad

The orange and ginger flavors complement each other. Serve with buns.

Boneless, skinless chicken breast halves (about 2), sliced paper-thin	½ lb.	225 g
Juice of 1 medium orange		
Finely grated peel of 1 medium orange		
Low-sodium soy sauce	1 tbsp.	15 mL
Grated gingerroot	2 tsp.	10 mL
Frozen concentrated orange juice	2 tbsp.	30 mL
Ground ginger	1 tsp.	5 mL
Garlic powder	⅛ tsp.	0.5 mL
Ginger ale	½ cup	125 mL
Cornstarch	1 tsp.	5 mL
Cooked bow tie (medium) pasta (farfalle), about 1 cup (250 mL), uncooked	2 cups	500 mL
Medium carrot, thinly peeled lengthwise into long ribbons	1	1
Green onion, sliced	1	1
Thinly sliced celery, cut on the diagonal	½ cup	125 mL
Finely shredded red cabbage	1 cup	250 mL
Medium orange or yellow peppers, slivered	2	2

Place first 5 ingredients in small bowl. Stir. Let stand for 15 minutes. Heat non-stick skillet or wok. Add chicken mixture. Stir-fry for 10 minutes until chicken is no longer pink and most of liquid is evaporated.

Combine next 5 ingredients in small cup. Stir. Add to chicken mixture. Stir until mixture comes to a boil. Boil for 1 minute until slightly thickened. Remove from heat. Cool.

Combine remaining 6 ingredients in large bowl. Add chicken mixture. Stir well. Serve immediately or chill until cold. Makes 6 cups (1.5 L).

1 cup (250 mL): 158 Calories; 1 g Total Fat (0.2 g Sat., 21.8 mg Cholesterol); 148 mg Sodium; 12 g Protein; 27 g Carbohydrate; 4 g Dietary Fiber

Pictured on page 90.

Artichoke Salad

To save time, cook pasta while preparing vegetables.

TOMATO VINAIGRETTE

Tomato juice	1 cup	250 mL
White wine vinegar	3 tbsp.	50 mL
Basil Pesto, page 78 (or commercial)	1 tbsp.	15 mL
Pectin granules	1 tbsp.	15 mL
Granulated sugar	½ tsp.	2 mL

SALAD

Rotini (spiral pasta), 4 oz. (113 g)	1½ cups	375 mL
Fresh (or frozen or dried) cheese-filled tortellini	4 oz.	113 g
Boiling water	3 qts.	3 L
Salt	1 tbsp.	15 mL
Canned artichoke hearts, drained and quartered	14 oz.	398 mL
Ripe pitted olives, drained and chopped	2 tbsp.	30 mL
Medium red pepper, finely chopped	½	½
Medium red onion, finely chopped	½	½
Medium carrot, grated	1	1
Grated light Parmesan cheese product	1 tbsp.	15 mL
Romaine lettuce leaves, to cover individual plates		
Medium tomatoes, cut into wedges	2	2
Toasted pine nuts (optional)	2 tbsp.	30 mL

Tomato Vinaigrette: Combine all 5 ingredients in jar. Cover. Shake well. Let stand at room temperature for 20 minutes until slightly thickened. Makes about 1¼ cups (300 mL) vinaigrette.

Salad: Cook both pastas in boiling water and salt in Dutch oven for 10 minutes, stirring occasionally, until tender but firm. Drain. Rinse with cold water. Drain.

Combine next 6 ingredients in large bowl. Add vinaigrette and pasta. Toss well.

Arrange lettuce leaves on individual plates. Divide salad over leaves. Garnish with tomato wedges and pine nuts. Makes 7 cups (1.75 L).

1 cup (250 mL): 150 Calories; 3.3 g Total Fat (0.4 g Sat., 10.2 mg Cholesterol); 315 mg Sodium; 6 g Protein; 25 g Carbohydrate; 3 g Dietary Fiber

Pictured on page 107.

Prosciutto And Melon Salad

Prosciutto (proh-SHOO-toh) is the Italian word for "ham."
It is ham that has been seasoned, salt-cured and air-dried.

Tubetti (very small tube pasta)	1⅓ cups	325 mL
Boiling water	6 cups	1.5 L
Salt	1½ tsp.	7 mL
Lean prosciutto ham, trimmed of fat and finely chopped	3 oz.	85 g
Medium cantaloupe, peeled and diced (2 cups, 500 mL)	½	½
Finely chopped red onion	¼ cup	60 mL
Chopped fresh parsley	¼ cup	60 mL
Non-fat sour cream	½ cup	125 mL
Skim evaporated milk	⅓ cup	75 mL
Liquid honey	2 tbsp.	30 mL
Dijon mustard	1 tbsp.	15 mL
Finely grated lemon peel	¾ tsp.	4 mL
Salt	⅛ tsp.	0.5 mL

Freshly ground pepper, sprinkle

Cook pasta in boiling water and first amount of salt in medium saucepan for about 8 minutes, stirring occasionally, until tender but firm. Drain. Rinse with cold water. Drain. Place in medium bowl.

Add prosciutto, cantaloupe, red onion and parsley.

Combine next 6 ingredients in small bowl. Whisk until smooth. Pour over pasta mixture. Mix well.

Sprinkle with pepper. Chill. Makes 5 cups (1.25 L).

1 cup (250 mL): 223 Calories; 3.2 g Total Fat (0.9 g Sat., 17.7 mg Cholesterol); 631 mg Sodium; 13 g Protein; 36 g Carbohydrate; 1 g Dietary Fiber

Pictured on page 35.

Variation: Lean ham (or other lean cold cuts) can be substituted for prosciutto if desired.

To fit long string pasta (such as spaghetti or fettuccine) into a saucepan of boiling water without having to break it up, hold in a bunch and place one end in the water. As pasta begins to soften, bend slightly and gradually lower into water. Be careful not to burn yourself with the steam.

104

Coconut Curry Sauce

Lovely yellow color with bits of onion and basil showing. Very flavorful sauce!

Brown sugar, packed	1 tbsp.	15 mL
Cornstarch	1½ tbsp.	25 mL
Medium unsweetened coconut	⅓ cup	75 mL
Skim evaporated milk	13½ oz.	385 mL
Garlic cloves, minced	2	2
Minced gingerroot	1 tbsp.	15 mL
Chopped onion	¼ cup	60 mL
Sesame oil	½ tsp.	2 mL
Vegetable oil	½ tsp.	2 mL
Canned diced green chilies, drained	4 oz.	114 mL
Chopped fresh sweet basil (or 2 tsp., 10 mL, dried)	2 tbsp.	30 mL
Juice and grated peel of 1 small lemon		
Ground coriander	1 tsp.	5 mL
Turmeric	½ tsp.	2 mL
Salt	½ tsp.	2 mL
Coconut flavoring	½ tsp.	2 mL
Cooked shrimp (or chicken)	8 oz.	225 g

Combine brown sugar, cornstarch and coconut in small saucepan. Slowly add evaporated milk. Cook, stirring frequently, until boiling and slightly thickened. Cool slightly.

Sauté garlic, ginger and onion in both oils in small non-stick skillet for about 2 minutes until onion is soft but not brown.

Stir in green chilies, basil, lemon juice and peel. Cook until most of liquid is absorbed.

Stir in coriander, turmeric and salt. Mix well. Remove from heat.

Place milk mixture and onion mixture in blender. Process. Add coconut flavoring. Process until almost smooth. Pour into medium saucepan. Add shrimp. Stir to warm. Makes about 3 cups (750 mL).

½ cup (125 mL): 163 Calories; 4.9 g Total Fat (3.3 g Sat., 75.6 mg Cholesterol); 394 mg Sodium; 14 g Protein; 17 g Carbohydrate; 1 g Dietary Fiber

Pictured on page 89.

 To serve sauces, place cooked pasta in a large, wide pasta bowl and pour sauce into the center. Or, toss pasta and sauce together and mound in the bowl. Serve with pasta tongs or a pasta fork and make sure everyone has their own pasta bowl.

Hunan Chicken Sauce

This has a spicy bite to it. Preparation time is 20 minutes.

Large onion, coarsely chopped	1	1
Chili oil	1 tsp.	5 mL
Garlic cloves, minced	2	2
Minced gingerroot	1 tbsp.	15 mL
Boneless, skinless chicken breast halves (about 2), diced into ½ inch (12 mm) cubes	½ lb.	225 g
Large red pepper, diced	1	1
Condensed chicken broth	10 oz.	284 mL
Chili sauce	¼ cup	60 mL
Hoisin sauce	1 tbsp.	15 mL
Low-sodium soy sauce	1 tbsp.	15 mL
Granulated sugar	2 tsp.	10 mL
Dried crushed chilies	⅛ -¼ tsp.	0.5-1 mL
Water	2 tbsp.	30 mL
Sherry (or alcohol-free sherry)	2 tbsp.	30 mL
Rice vinegar	2 tbsp.	30 mL
Cornstarch	3 tbsp.	50 mL

Sauté onion in oil in large non-stick skillet or wok until soft. Add garlic and ginger. Sauté for 30 seconds.

Add chicken. Stir-fry for 2 minutes. Stir in red pepper. Add next 6 ingredients. Bring to a boil. Simmer, uncovered, for 5 minutes.

Combine remaining 4 ingredients in small bowl. Stir into chicken mixture. Heat until boiling and thickened. Makes 4 cups (1 L).

½ cup (125 mL): 94 Calories; 1.4 g Total Fat (0.3 g Sat., 16.7 mg Cholesterol); 546 mg Sodium; 9 g Protein; 11 g Carbohydrate; 1 g Dietary Fiber

Pictured on page 89.

1. Artichoke Salad, page 103
2. Fruity Turkey Salad, page 100
3. Pasta Bean Salad, page 96
4. Tortellini And Tzatziki Salad, page 94

Props Courtesy Of: Stokes

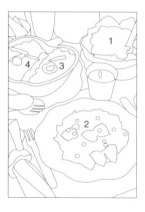

Roasted Pepper And Tomato Sauce

*Great over any pasta. Use as an alternative second
sauce when serving cream-based sauces.*

Large red peppers	4	4
Garlic cloves, minced	3	3
Finely minced onion	2 tbsp.	30 mL
Olive oil	1 tbsp.	15 mL
Canned crushed tomatoes	14 oz.	398 mL
Chopped fresh sweet basil (or 1 tsp., 5 mL, dried)	1 tbsp.	15 mL
Salt	½ tsp.	2 mL
Freshly ground pepper, sprinkle		

Place red peppers on baking sheet with sides. Broil, turning often, for 15 to
20 minutes until skin is blackened. Place in small bowl. Cover with plastic wrap
for 15 to 20 minutes until cool enough to handle. Peel skin from pepper,
reserving any liquid. Strain reserved liquid. Discard seeds and membrane.

Sauté garlic and onion in oil in large saucepan until garlic is golden and onion
is soft.

Process red peppers with reserved liquid and tomato in 2 batches, until smooth.
Add to saucepan.

Stir in basil, salt and pepper. Cover. Simmer for about 10 minutes. Makes
3²/₃ cups (900 mL).

*½ **cup (125 mL)**: 42 Calories; 2.1 g Total Fat (0.3 g Sat., 0 mg Cholesterol); 276 mg Sodium;
1 g Protein; 6 g Carbohydrate; 1 g Dietary Fiber*

Pictured on page 144.

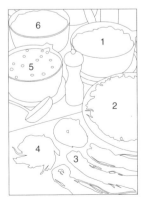

1. Clams In Wine Sauce, page 116
2. Whole Wheat Pasta Dough, page 85
3. Green Onion Pasta Dough, page 83
4. Chili Pepper Pasta Dough, page 82
5. Mint Green Pea Sauce, page 116
6. Creamed Spinach Sauce, page 112

Props Courtesy Of: Eaton's
                    Stokes

Easy Spicy Tomato Sauce

The name says it all—easy and spicy. Only ten minutes preparation time.

Olive oil	1 tsp.	5 mL
Finely diced onion	1 cup	250 mL
Garlic cloves, minced	2	2
Chili powder	1/2 tsp.	2 mL
Dried crushed chilies	1/8-1/4 tsp.	0.5-1 mL
Canned plum tomatoes, with juice, processed	28 oz.	796 mL
Granulated sugar	1/8 tsp.	0.5 mL

Heat oil in large non-stick skillet. Sauté onion for 5 minutes. Add garlic, chili powder, chilies and 1 tbsp. (15 mL) processed tomato. Sauté for 5 minutes until onion is soft.

Add remaining tomato and sugar. Simmer, partially covered, for 10 minutes until slightly thickened. Makes 3 cups (750 mL).

1/2 cup (125 mL): 47 Calories; 1.2 g Total Fat (0.2 g Sat., 0 mg Cholesterol); 223 mg Sodium; 2 g Protein; 9 g Carbohydrate; 2 g Dietary Fiber

Pictured on page 143.

Mushroom Dill Sauce

Try using shiitake or portobello mushrooms to give this sauce an extra delicious flavor.

Diet tub margarine	1 tbsp.	15 mL
Finely chopped onion	1/4 cup	60 mL
Chopped fresh mushrooms	2 cups	500 mL
Water	1 cup	250 mL
Beef bouillon powder	2 tsp.	10 mL
Pepper	1/8 tsp.	0.5 mL
Skim evaporated milk	13 1/2 oz.	385 mL
All-purpose flour	1 tbsp.	15 mL
Non-fat spreadable cream cheese	8 oz.	225 g
Chopped fresh dill (or 1 tsp., 5 mL, dried)	1 tbsp.	15 mL

Melt margarine in large non-stick skillet. Sauté onion for 5 minutes until soft. Add mushrooms. Sauté for 5 minutes until liquid is evaporated. Stir in water, bouillon powder and pepper.

Combine evaporated milk and flour in small bowl. Mix. Add to mushroom mixture. Heat, stirring constantly, until boiling and slightly thickened. Remove from heat.

Add cream cheese. Stir until melted. Stir in dill. Makes 2 1/4 cups (560 mL).

1/2 cup (125 mL): 151 Calories; 1.9 g Total Fat (0.5 g Sat., 3.5 mg Cholesterol); 403 mg Sodium; 12 g Protein; 22 g Carbohydrate; 1 g Dietary Fiber

Creamy Peppered Chicken Sauce

This is terrific served over spinach fettuccine.

Boneless, skinless chicken breast halves (about 4), thinly sliced	1 lb.	454 g
Paprika	1 tsp.	5 mL
Coarsely ground pepper	1 tsp.	5 mL
Tub margarine	1 tsp.	5 mL
Hot water	1 cup	250 mL
Chicken bouillon powder	2 tsp.	10 mL
All-purpose flour	1 tbsp.	15 mL
Skim evaporated milk	½ cup	125 mL
Non-fat spreadable herb & garlic-flavored cream cheese	½ cup	125 mL
Granulated sugar	1 tsp.	5 mL
Salt	¼ tsp.	1 mL
Thinly slivered fresh sweet basil (or 2 tsp., 10 mL, dried)	2 tbsp.	30 mL
Chopped fresh parsley (or 2 tsp., 10 mL, dried)	2 tbsp.	30 mL
Non-fat plain yogurt	½ cup	125 mL

Combine chicken, paprika and pepper in small bowl. Cover. Chill for at least 20 minutes.

Melt margarine in medium non-stick skillet until bubbling. Add chicken. Sauté for 4 to 5 minutes until chicken is golden and no longer pink. Add hot water and bouillon powder. Stir. Bring to a boil.

Combine flour and evaporated milk in small cup. Mix until smooth. Add to chicken mixture. Stir until slightly thickened.

Add cream cheese, sugar and salt. Stir until melted. Remove from heat. Stir in basil, parsley and yogurt. Makes 3¾ cups (925 mL).

½ cup (125 mL): 120 Calories; 1.5 g Total Fat (0.4 g Sat., 36.2 mg Cholesterol); 344 mg Sodium; 18 g Protein; 8 g Carbohydrate; trace Dietary Fiber

Pictured on the front cover.

 Fresh tomatoes vary in acidity. Taste the finished sauce; if it is too tart, add a sprinkle of granulated sugar to cut acidity.

Creamed Spinach Sauce

Delicious flavor combination of wine, spinach and cheese. Only 20 minutes preparation time.

Garlic clove, minced	1	1
Diet tub margarine	1 tbsp.	15 mL
White (or alcohol-free white) wine	½ cup	125 mL
Firmly packed chopped fresh spinach (or 10 oz., 300 g, frozen chopped spinach, thawed and squeezed dry)	3 cups	750 mL
Light spreadable cream cheese	½ cup	125 mL
Skim evaporated milk	1 cup	250 mL
Cornstarch	2 tsp.	10 mL
Salt	½ tsp.	2 mL
Freshly ground pepper, sprinkle		
Ground nutmeg, sprinkle		

Sauté garlic in margarine in large non-stick skillet for 1 minute until soft. Add wine. Stir until boiling. Stir in spinach. Cover. Cook for 2 to 3 minutes. Add cream cheese. Stir until melted.

Combine evaporated milk and cornstarch in small bowl. Mix. Add to spinach mixture. Add salt, pepper and nutmeg. Cook until boiling and slightly thickened. Makes 2½ cups (625 mL).

½ cup (125 mL): 134 Calories; 5.5 g Total Fat (2.6 g Sat., 14.5 mg Cholesterol); 629 mg Sodium; 8 g Protein; 10 g Carbohydrate; 1 g Dietary Fiber

Pictured on page 108.

Garlic Shrimp And Vegetable Sauce

A delicate wine and seafood sauce.

White (or alcohol-free white) wine	½ cup	125 mL
Fresh (or frozen, thawed) uncooked shrimp, peeled and deveined	1 lb.	454 g
Garlic cloves, minced	3	3
Sliced fresh mushrooms	2 cups	500 mL
Hot water	½ cup	125 mL
Seafood (or vegetable) bouillon powder	1 tsp.	5 mL
Small broccoli florets	2 cups	500 mL
Salt	1 tsp.	5 mL
Pepper	⅛ tsp.	0.5 mL
Skim evaporated milk	1 cup	250 mL
Cornstarch	2 tbsp.	30 mL
Green onion, sliced	1	1

(continued on next page)

Heat wine in large non-stick skillet. Add shrimp and garlic. Sauté for about 2 minutes until shrimp is pink. Don't overcook. Remove shrimp to medium bowl with slotted spoon.

Add mushrooms to wine in skillet. Sauté for 3 minutes. Add hot water and bouillon powder. Bring to a boil. Add broccoli, salt and pepper. Cover. Cook for 1 to 2 minutes.

Stir evaporated milk and cornstarch together in small bowl. Add to liquid in skillet. Cook for 2 to 3 minutes until broccoli is tender-crisp and mixture is bubbling and thickened. Stir in shrimp and green onion. Makes 8 cups (2 L).

1/2 cup (125 mL): 59 Calories; 0.6 g Total Fat (0.1 g Sat., 43.8 mg Cholesterol); 272 mg Sodium; 8 g Protein; 4 g Carbohydrate; trace Dietary Fiber

Pictured on page 53.

Cold Mushroom Salsa

Chunky with a "fresh" taste. Can be kept in the refrigerator for up to two days. Bring to room temperature before serving. Toss with hot pasta.

Olive oil	1 tbsp.	15 mL
Garlic clove, minced	1	1
Fresh lemon juice	2 tbsp.	30 mL
Finely grated lemon peel	1 tsp.	5 mL
Non-fat Italian dressing	1/3 cup	75 mL
Chopped fresh parsley (or 2 tsp., 10 mL, dried)	2 tbsp.	30 mL
Chopped fresh oregano (or 1/2 tsp., 2 mL, dried)	2 tsp.	10 mL
Salt	1/2 tsp.	2 mL
Freshly ground pepper, sprinkle		
Finely chopped red pepper	1/4 cup	60 mL
Finely chopped red onion	1/4 cup	60 mL
Coarsely chopped fresh mushrooms	2 cups	500 mL

Combine first 9 ingredients in medium bowl.

Stir in red pepper, red onion and mushrooms. Cover. Marinate in refrigerator for at least 1 hour. Makes 1¾ cups (425 mL).

1/4 cup (60 mL): 33 Calories; 2.1 g Total Fat (0.3 g Sat., 0 mg Cholesterol); 330 mg Sodium; 1 g Protein; 3 g Carbohydrate; 1 g Dietary Fiber

Pictured on page 90.

Bolognese Sauce

A thick, full-bodied meat and vegetable sauce.

Lean ground beef	1 lb.	454 g
Chopped onion	2 cups	500 mL
Garlic cloves, crushed	2	2
Sliced fresh mushrooms	2 cups	500 mL
Salt	1 tsp.	5 mL
Pepper	1/4 tsp.	1 mL
Chopped fresh sweet basil (or 1 tbsp., 15 mL, dried)	1/4 cup	60 mL
Chopped fresh oregano (or 2 tsp., 10 mL, dried)	2 tbsp.	30 mL
Canned plum tomatoes, with juice, crushed or processed	28 oz.	796 mL
Tomato paste	5 1/2 oz.	156 mL
Granulated sugar	1/2 tsp.	2 mL
Water	3 cups	750 mL

Scramble-fry ground beef, onion and garlic in non-stick skillet until beef is browned and onion is soft. Drain.

Add mushrooms, salt and pepper. Sauté for 5 minutes. Pour into large saucepan.

Add remaining 6 ingredients. Bring to a boil. Simmer, uncovered, for 1 1/2 hours, stirring occasionally, until thickened. Makes 6 cups (1.5 L).

1/2 cup (125 mL): 100 Calories; 3.6 g Total Fat (1.3 g Sat., 19.5 mg Cholesterol); 361 mg Sodium; 9 g Protein; 9 g Carbohydrate; 2 g Dietary Fiber

Pictured on page 144.

Cold Garlic Cream Sauce

Smooth sauce with a strong garlic flavor. Try the variations for a more herbal taste.

Non-fat sour cream	2/3 cup	150 mL
Non-fat salad dressing (or mayonnaise)	1/3 cup	75 mL
Skim milk	3 tbsp.	50 mL
White (or alcohol-free white) wine	3 tbsp.	50 mL
Lemon juice	1 tbsp.	15 mL
Granulated sugar	2 tsp.	10 mL
Salt	1 tsp.	5 mL
Garlic cloves, minced	5	5

(continued on next page)

Whisk all 8 ingredients together in small bowl until smooth. Chill for at least 1 hour to allow flavors to meld. Spoon about 2 tbsp. (30 mL) sauce per serving over hot pasta. Makes 1½ cups (375 mL).

2 tbsp. (30 mL): 20 Calories; trace Total Fat (trace Sat., 0.1 mg Cholesterol); 279 mg Sodium; 1 g Protein; 3 g Carbohydrate; trace Dietary Fiber

Pictured on page 143.

Variations:

1. Add 1½ tbsp. (25 mL) chopped fresh sweet basil or 1 tsp. (5 mL) dried.

2. Add 1½ tbsp. (25 mL) chopped fresh oregano or 1 tsp. (5 mL) dried.

3. Add 1½ tbsp. (25 mL) chopped fresh dill or 1 tsp. (5 mL) dried.

Zucchini And Mushroom Sauce

This chunky sauce is perfect for string, spiral or medium-size pasta. Only 15 minutes preparation time.

Quartered fresh mushrooms	4 cups	1 L
Garlic cloves, minced	3	3
Olive oil	1 tsp.	5 mL
Diced zucchini, with peel (¾ inch, 2 cm, pieces)	3 cups	750 mL
Olive oil	1 tsp.	5 mL
Canned stewed tomatoes, processed	14 oz.	398 mL
Dried sweet basil, crushed	1 tsp.	5 mL
Dried whole oregano, crushed	½ tsp.	2 mL
Salt	½ tsp.	2 mL
Freshly ground pepper, sprinkle		
Skim evaporated milk	½ cup	125 mL

Sauté mushrooms and garlic in first amount of oil in large non-stick skillet for about 10 minutes until liquid is evaporated and mushrooms are golden. Remove to small bowl.

In same skillet, sauté zucchini in second amount of oil for about 5 minutes until zucchini is soft but not mushy. Return mushrooms to skillet.

Stir in tomato, basil, oregano, salt and pepper. Boil for 2 to 3 minutes.

Remove from heat. Add evaporated milk. Stir. Makes 5 cups (1.25 L).

⅔ cup (150 mL): 60 Calories; 1.6 g Total Fat (0.2 g Sat., 0.6 mg Cholesterol); 350 mg Sodium; 3 g Protein; 10 g Carbohydrate; 2 g Dietary Fiber

Pictured on page 144.

Clams In Wine Sauce

Not a thick sauce, but perfect to smother pasta in. Garnish with fresh parsley.

Canned baby clams, drained and juice reserved	2 × 5 oz.	2 × 142 g
White wine	¼ cup	60 mL
Green onions, sliced	2	2
Dried sweet basil	1 tsp.	5 mL
Dried whole oregano, crushed	¼ tsp.	1 mL
Dried rosemary, crushed	¼ tsp.	1 mL
Sliced fresh mushrooms	1 cup	250 mL
Skim evaporated milk	1 cup	250 mL
Cornstarch	4 tsp.	20 mL
Non-fat spreadable cream cheese	2 tbsp.	30 mL

Combine juice from clams, wine, green onion, basil, oregano, rosemary and mushrooms in medium saucepan. Cover. Simmer for 15 minutes until mushrooms are soft.

Combine evaporated milk and cornstarch in small bowl. Add to mushroom mixture. Stir until boiling and thickened. Stir in clams. Simmer until hot. Remove from heat.

Add cream cheese. Stir until melted. Makes 3 cups (750 mL).

½ cup (125 mL): 101 Calories; 0.7 g Total Fat (0.1 g Sat., 22 mg Cholesterol); 194 mg Sodium; 11 g Protein; 10 g Carbohydrate; trace Dietary Fiber

Pictured on page 108.

Mint Green Pea Sauce

Serve over cooked Lemon Pepper Pasta, page 84, or your favorite pasta.

Condensed chicken broth	10 oz.	284 mL
Water	½ cup	125 mL
Fresh (or frozen, thawed) peas	1½ cups	375 mL
Green onions, cut on the diagonal into ½ inch (12 mm) thick slices	3	3
White (or alcohol-free white) wine	¼ cup	60 mL
Cornstarch	4 tsp.	20 mL
Chopped fresh mint leaves (or 1½ tsp., 7 mL, dried)	¼ cup	60 mL

(continued on next page)

Sauces

Combine chicken broth and water in medium saucepan. Bring to a boil. Add peas and green onion. Simmer, uncovered, for 2 to 3 minutes.

Combine wine and cornstarch in small cup. Mix. Add to pea mixture. Stir until boiling and slightly thickened. Remove from heat. Stir in mint. Makes 2¼ cups (560 mL).

½ cup (125 mL): 80 Calories; 0.9 g Total Fat (0.2 g Sat., 0.7 mg Cholesterol); 479 mg Sodium; 6 g Protein; 10 g Carbohydrate; 3 g Dietary Fiber

Pictured on page 108.

Tomato Meatball Sauce

A perfect sauce if you're in the mood for spaghetti and meatballs!

Canned stewed tomatoes, with juice, chopped	28 oz.	796 mL
Tomato sauce	14 oz.	398 mL
Finely chopped onion	2 tbsp.	30 mL
Garlic cloves, minced	2	2
Whole cloves	10	10
Bay leaf	1	1
Dried sweet basil	1 tsp.	5 mL
Salt	½ tsp.	2 mL
Freshly ground pepper, sprinkle		
Lean ground beef	1 lb.	454 g
Bread slices, processed into crumbs	2	2
Frozen egg product, thawed	3 tbsp.	50 mL
Skim milk	⅓ cup	75 mL
Grated light Parmesan cheese product	2 tbsp.	30 mL
Garlic powder	½ tsp.	2 mL
Dried whole oregano, crushed	½ tsp.	2 mL
Salt, sprinkle		
Freshly ground pepper, sprinkle		

Combine first 9 ingredients in large saucepan. Bring to a boil. Reduce heat. Simmer, partially covered, for 45 minutes.

Combine remaining 9 ingredients in medium bowl. Mix well. Form into 1 inch (2.5 cm) balls. Place on lightly greased baking sheet with sides. Bake in 400°F (205°C) oven for about 15 minutes. Drain. Blot meatballs with paper towel. Add meatballs to sauce. Simmer, partially covered, for 30 minutes. Discard bay leaf and cloves. Makes 6 cups (1.5 L) sauce with meatballs.

¾ cup (175 mL): 163 Calories; 5.5 g Total Fat (2.1 g Sat., 30.3 mg Cholesterol); 896 mg Sodium; 14 g Protein; 16 g Carbohydrate; 2 g Dietary Fiber

Herbed Tomato Soup

Rich red color. Lots of delicious tomato chunks. Only ten minutes preparation time.

Finely chopped onion	½ cup	125 mL
Garlic cloves, minced	2	2
Olive oil	1 tsp.	5 mL
Fennel seed	½ tsp.	2 mL
Ripe medium plum tomatoes, diced	3	3
Canned plum tomatoes, with juice, processed	28 oz.	796 mL
Condensed chicken broth	10 oz.	284 mL
Water	1½ cups	375 mL
Minced fresh sweet basil (or 1 tsp., 5 mL, dried)	1 tbsp.	15 mL
Minced fresh marjoram (or ½ tsp., 2 mL, dried)	1½ tsp.	7 mL
Minced fresh oregano (or ¼ tsp., 1 mL, dried)	1 tsp.	5 mL
Granulated sugar	½ tsp.	2 mL
Uncooked orzo (very small pasta)	⅔ cup	150 mL
Grated light Parmesan cheese product, sprinkle (optional)		
Freshly ground pepper, sprinkle (optional)		

Sauté onion and garlic in oil in non-stick skillet until onion is soft. Add fennel seed. Sauté for 1 minute.

Add next 8 ingredients. Cover. Simmer for 30 to 40 minutes.

Add pasta. Simmer, uncovered, for 10 to 12 minutes, stirring occasionally, until pasta is tender but firm.

Sprinkle with Parmesan cheese and pepper. Makes 7 cups (1.75 L).

1 cup (250 mL): 150 Calories; 2 g Total Fat (0.4 g Sat., 0.4 mg Cholesterol); 465 mg Sodium; 7 g Protein; 27 g Carbohydrate; 3 g Dietary Fiber

Pictured on page 90.

 Only a small amount of pasta left in a bag? Collect leftover same-size pasta shapes in a jar or airtight container and mix together to use in everyday pasta dishes and soups.

Zuppa Fagioli

Fagioli (faj-YOH-lee) is the Italian word for "beans."
A hearty Italian meal-in-one bean soup. Only 20 minutes preparation time.

Olive oil	1 tsp.	5 mL
Extra lean ground beef	1/2 lb.	225 g
Chopped onion	1 cup	250 mL
Chopped white celery heart (use inside ribs with leaves)	1 cup	250 mL
Medium carrot, grated	1	1
Large garlic clove, minced	1	1
Canned plum tomatoes, processed	28 oz.	796 mL
Canned white kidney beans, with liquid	19 oz.	540 mL
Canned beans in tomato sauce, with liquid	14 oz.	398 mL
Liquid beef bouillon concentrate	2 tsp.	10 mL
Tomato paste	2 tbsp.	30 mL
Dried sweet basil	2 tsp.	10 mL
Dried whole oregano	1/4 tsp.	1 mL
Dried thyme	1/4 tsp.	1 mL
Dried crushed chilies	1/4 tsp.	1 mL
Salt	1/2 tsp.	2 mL
Pepper	1/8 tsp.	0.5 mL
Granulated sugar	1/2 tsp.	2 mL
Water	3 cups	750 mL
Uncooked tubetti (very small tube pasta)	1 cup	250 mL
Freshly ground pepper, sprinkle		

Heat oil in large Dutch oven. Scramble-fry next 5 ingredients until beef is browned and vegetables are tender-crisp. Drain.

Add next 12 ingredients. Stir well.

Add water. Cover. Bring to a boil. Reduce heat and simmer for 1 hour.

Stir in pasta. Simmer for 10 to 15 minutes until pasta is cooked.

Grind pepper over individual servings. Makes 12 cups (3 L).

1 cup (250 mL): 180 Calories; 3.8 g Total Fat (1.3 g Sat., 12.9 mg Cholesterol); 660 mg Sodium; 11 g Protein; 27 g Carbohydrate; 7 g Dietary Fiber

Pictured on the front cover.

 It takes a long time for water to reach its boiling point, so start heating the large pot of water for the pasta before you start preparations. Keep lid on to speed the process.

Lentil And Pasta Soup

A robust, hearty soup with lots of texture. About 20 minutes preparation time.

Garlic cloves, minced	2	2
Finely chopped onion	1 cup	250 mL
Chopped celery	1 cup	250 mL
Olive oil	2 tsp.	10 mL
Water	7 cups	1.75 L
Beef (or chicken) bouillon powder	2 tbsp.	30 mL
Canned tomatoes, with juice, processed	14 oz.	398 mL
Thinly sliced carrot	1½ cups	375 mL
Green lentils	¾ cup	175 mL
Parsley flakes	2 tsp.	10 mL
Dried sweet basil	1 tsp.	5 mL
Salt	1 tsp.	5 mL
Ground oregano, pinch		
Pepper, sprinkle		
Tubetti (very small pasta)	1 cup	250 mL

Sauté garlic, onion and celery in oil in Dutch oven until onion is soft.

Add next 10 ingredients. Bring mixture to a boil. Simmer, partially covered, for 30 minutes.

Stir in pasta. Simmer for 15 minutes. Makes about 8 cups (2 L).

1 cup (250 mL): 158 Calories; 2 g Total Fat (0.4 g Sat., 0.3 mg Cholesterol); 893 mg Sodium; 8 g Protein; 28 g Carbohydrate; 4 g Dietary Fiber

Pictured on page 89.

Lemon Pesto Soup

A very refreshing soup. Only ten minutes preparation time.

Condensed chicken broth	3 × 10 oz.	3 × 284 mL
Water	3 cups	750 mL
Basil Pesto, page 78 (or commercial)	1 tbsp.	15 mL
Uncooked tubetti (very small tube pasta)	¾ cup	175 mL
Fresh lemon juice	2 tbsp.	30 mL
Large eggs	2	2
Chopped fresh parsley	¼ cup	60 mL
Salt, just a pinch		
Pepper, sprinkle		

(continued on next page)

120 Soups

Combine chicken broth, water and pesto in large saucepan. Bring to a boil.

Add pasta. Stir well. Simmer, uncovered, for 3 minutes.

Beat lemon juice and eggs together in small bowl. Remove some hot broth mixture with ladle and stir into egg mixture. Slowly add egg mixture to soup, stirring constantly. Remove from heat. Cover. Let stand for 5 minutes.

Stir in parsley, salt and pepper. Makes 7 cups (1.75 L).

1 cup (250 mL): 135 Calories; 4.2 g Total Fat (1.1 g Sat., 63.1 mg Cholesterol); 837 mg Sodium; 10 g Protein; 14 g Carbohydrate; 1 g Dietary Fiber

Variation: Substitute chopped fresh mint for parsley.

Hearty Zucchini Chowder

Thick and creamy with a subtle dill taste. Only 20 minutes to prepare vegetables.

Small garlic clove, minced	1	1
Chopped onion	1 cup	250 mL
Chopped celery	1/2 cup	125 mL
Chopped green pepper	1/2 cup	125 mL
Tub margarine	1 tsp.	5 mL
Grated zucchini, with peel	2 cups	500 mL
Diced potato	2 cups	500 mL
Water	6 cups	1.5 L
Vegetable (or chicken) bouillon powder	2 tbsp.	30 mL
Uncooked tubetti (very small pasta)	1 cup	250 mL
Dill weed	1 tsp.	5 mL
Salt	1/2 tsp.	2 mL
Pepper	1/8 - 1/4 tsp.	0.5-1 mL
All-purpose flour	3 tbsp.	50 mL
Skim evaporated milk	1 cup	250 mL

Sauté garlic, onion, celery and green pepper in margarine in Dutch oven for about 3 minutes until vegetables are soft.

Add next 4 ingredients. Simmer, partially covered, for 20 minutes.

Stir in pasta, dill weed, salt and pepper. Simmer for 10 to 15 minutes, stirring occasionally, until pasta is tender but firm.

Whisk flour and evaporated milk together in small bowl until smooth. Add to soup, stirring continually, until mixture boils. Makes 9 cups (2.25 L).

1 cup (250 mL): 126 Calories; 1 g Total Fat (0.3 g Sat., 1.3 mg Cholesterol); 598 mg Sodium; 6 g Protein; 24 g Carbohydrate; 2 g Dietary Fiber

Pictured on page 125.

Creamed Broccoli Soup

Cayenne pepper gives this soup a bit of bite. Only 20 minutes preparation time.

Chopped onion	²/₃ cup	150 mL
Clove garlic, minced	1	1
Diet tub margarine	1 tsp.	5 mL
Brown sugar, packed	1 tsp.	5 mL
Condensed chicken broth	2 × 10 oz.	2 × 284 mL
Water	2 cups	500 mL
Bay leaf	1	1
Cayenne pepper, sprinkle		
Seasoning salt	1 tsp.	5 mL
Broccoli, chopped (reserve 1 cup, 250 mL, florets)	2 lbs.	900 g
Skim evaporated milk	1 cup	250 mL
All-purpose flour	2 tbsp.	30 mL
Reserved chopped broccoli florets	1 cup	250 mL
Spaghetti (string pasta), broken into 2 inch (5 cm) lengths (see Note)	2 oz.	57 g
Boiling water	4 cups	1 L

Sauté onion and garlic in margarine in large saucepan until onion is soft. Sprinkle with brown sugar. Stir. Cook, stirring often, until onion is golden and very soft.

Stir in chicken broth, water, bay leaf, cayenne pepper and seasoning salt. Add broccoli. Bring to a boil. Cover. Simmer for 30 to 40 minutes until broccoli is tender. Discard bay leaf. Remove broccoli to blender with slotted spoon. Process until smooth. Return to broth mixture in saucepan. Bring to a boil.

Combine evaporated milk and flour in small bowl. Mix until smooth. Stir into soup. Add reserved broccoli florets. Boil until broccoli is tender-crisp and soup is thickened.

Cook pasta in boiling water (no salt added) in large saucepan for 10 minutes, stirring occasionally, until tender but firm. Drain. Add to soup. Makes 6 cups (1.5 L)

1 cup (250 mL): 167 Calories; 2.2 g Total Fat (0.5 g Sat., 2.6 mg Cholesterol); 958 mg Sodium; 14 g Protein; 25 g Carbohydrate; 4 g Dietary Fiber

Pictured on page 125.

Note: The same amount of Lemon Pepper Pasta, page 84, cut into string pasta, can be substituted to add zip.

 You can increase the quantity of any cream or clear soup by adding a handful of small or very small pasta, simmering until tender.

Summertime Soup

*If you wish, use about 2 cups (500 mL) leftover cooked pasta
to replace the vermicelli. Sprinkle Parmesan cheese and fresh
sweet basil over each serving if desired.*

Chopped onion	1 cup	250 mL
Garlic cloves, minced	4	4
Olive oil	2 tsp.	10 mL
Chopped celery	½ cup	125 mL
Diced carrot	½ cup	125 mL
Diced potato	1 cup	250 mL
Young fresh green beans, cut into ¾ inch (2 cm) lengths	1 cup	250 mL
Canned diced tomatoes, with juice	14 oz.	398 mL
Dried sweet basil	4 tsp.	20 mL
Seasoning salt	1½ tsp.	7 mL
Ground marjoram	½ tsp.	2 mL
Ground pepper	⅛ tsp.	0.5 mL
Bay leaves	2	2
Water	8 cups	2 L
Cooked small white beans (navy beans), with liquid	14 oz.	398 mL
Slivered fresh spinach, packed	2 cups	500 mL
Vermicelli (thin string pasta), broken into 2 inch (5 cm) lengths	4 oz.	113 g
Boiling water	1 qt.	1 L
Salt	1 tsp.	5 mL

Sauté onion and garlic in oil in Dutch oven for about 5 minutes, stirring
frequently, until onion is soft.

Add next 11 ingredients. Bring to a boil. Reduce heat. Simmer, partially covered,
for 15 minutes until potato is almost cooked.

Add white beans and spinach. Simmer, uncovered, for 5 to 6 minutes until
potato and green beans are tender. Discard bay leaves.

Cook pasta in boiling water and salt in medium saucepan for 5 minutes, stirring
occasionally, until just tender. Drain. Stir into soup. Makes 13 cups (3.25 L).

*1 cup (250 mL): 109 Calories; 1.1 g Total Fat (0.2 g Sat., 0 mg Cholesterol); 224 mg Sodium;
5 g Protein; 21 g Carbohydrate; 3 g Dietary Fiber*

Pictured on page 125.

Pasta And Cabbage Soup

A thick, hearty soup. Very quick and easy to prepare.

Chopped onion	1 cup	250 mL
Olive oil	1 tsp.	5 mL
Thinly shredded green cabbage	4 cups	1 L
Water	2½ qts.	2.5 L
Canned stewed tomatoes, with liquid, chopped	14 oz.	398 mL
Medium carrot, coarsely grated	1	1
Vegetable bouillon powder	3 tbsp.	50 mL
Ground oregano	⅛ tsp.	0.5 mL
Pepper	⅛ tsp.	0.5 mL
Peeled and diced potato	2 cups	500 mL
Uncooked orzo (very small pasta)	⅔ cup	150 mL
Chopped fresh parsley	2 tbsp.	30 mL

Sauté onion in oil in Dutch oven for 3 to 4 minutes until soft. Stir in cabbage. Cook for about 5 minutes, stirring often, until cabbage is wilted.

Add water, tomato, carrot, bouillon powder, oregano and pepper. Bring mixture to a boil. Simmer, partially covered, for 20 minutes.

Add potato and pasta. Simmer, partially covered, for 15 minutes until potato is cooked and pasta is tender but firm.

Stir in parsley. Makes 12 cups (3 L).

1 cup (250 mL): 74 Calories; 0.9 g Total Fat (0.2 g Sat., 0.3 mg Cholesterol); 546 mg Sodium; 3 g Protein; 15 g Carbohydrate; 2 g Dietary Fiber

Pictured on page 125.

1. Summertime Soup, page 123
2. Pasta And Cabbage Soup, above
3. Creamed Broccoli Soup, page 122
4. Asparagus Leek Soup, page 131
5. Hearty Zucchini Chowder, page 121

Props Courtesy Of: Chintz & Company
Eaton's
Stokes

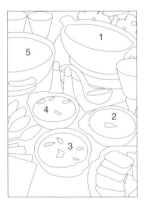

Wonton Soup

Slight hint of ginger.

Condensed chicken broth	2 × 10 oz.	2 × 284 mL
Water	5 cups	1.25 L
Low-sodium soy sauce	1 tbsp.	15 mL
Thin slice gingerroot	1	1
Bok choy, thinly sliced with green leaves	1 cup	250 mL
Thinly sliced fresh mushrooms (see Note)	1 cup	250 mL
Slivered cooked chicken, ham or pork (optional)	1/2 cup	125 mL
Canned sliced water chestnuts (optional)	1/2 × 8 oz.	1/2 × 227 mL
Crunchy Vegetarian Wontons, page 145, or Shrimp And Meat Wontons, page 142	25	25
Green onions, thinly sliced	2	2

Simmer broth, water, soy sauce, ginger slice and bok choy in Dutch oven for 5 minutes. Discard ginger slice.

Add mushrooms, meat and water chestnuts. Simmer for 5 minutes. Increase heat. Add wontons. Stir gently until boiling. Boil gently for 4 to 5 minutes until wontons are tender.

Add green onion. Serve immediately. Makes 8 cups (2 L).

1 cup (250 mL) plus wontons: 55 Calories; 1 g Total Fat (0.3 g Sat., 1.6 mg Cholesterol); 666 mg Sodium; 5 g Protein; 7 g Carbohydrate; 1 g Dietary Fiber

Note: Try shiitake or other exotic mushrooms for more flavor.

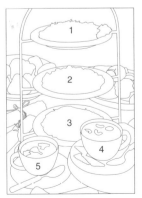

1. Pasta And Ceci, page 63
2. Gnocchi With Tomato Purée, page 80
3. Zucchini Pesto Sauté, page 60
4. Italian Minestrone, page 130
5. Tortellini In Broth, page 128

Props Courtesy Of: Chintz & Company
Creations By Design
Eaton's
Stokes

Leek And Potato Soup

Use up leftover scraps of fresh pasta such as Green Onion Pasta Dough, page 83, or Basil And Garlic Pasta Dough, page 82, in this creamy soup.

Medium leeks, thinly sliced	2	2
Diet tub margarine	1 tbsp.	15 mL
Water	8 cups	2 L
Diced peeled potato	3 cups	750 mL
Salt	1 tsp.	5 mL
Pepper, sprinkle		
Uncooked medium pasta (4 oz., 113 g)	1 cup	250 mL
Chopped fresh dill (or 2 tsp., 10 mL, dried)	2 tbsp.	30 mL
Skim evaporated milk	½ cup	125 mL

Sauté leeks in margarine in large saucepan until soft.

Add water, potato, salt and pepper. Bring to a boil. Reduce heat. Simmer, partially covered, for 10 minutes until potato is almost tender.

Stir in pasta and dill. Cook, partially covered, for 5 to 6 minutes for fresh pasta scraps, or for 8 to 10 minutes for dried pasta.

Add evaporated milk. Stir until heated through. Makes 8 cups (2 L).

1 cup (250 mL): 138 Calories; 1.1 g Total Fat (0.2 g Sat., 0.6 mg Cholesterol); 387 mg Sodium; 5 g Protein; 28 g Carbohydrate; 2 g Dietary Fiber

Tortellini In Broth

Homemade tortellini makes this soup exceptional, but if time is short, commercial tortellini is also great! Very quick and easy to prepare.

Condensed chicken broth	3 × 10 oz.	3 × 284 mL
Water	3½ cups	875 mL
Broccoli florets	2 cups	500 mL
Green onions, thinly sliced	4	4
Mushroom-Filled Tortellini, page 148	50	50
(½ of recipe), or 1 lb., 454 g,		
commercial cheese or meat-filled		
tortellini (see Note)		
Grated light Parmesan cheese product,		
sprinkle (optional)		

(continued on next page)

Bring chicken broth and water to a boil in Dutch oven.

Add broccoli and green onion. Simmer, partially covered, for 4 to 5 minutes. Add fresh tortellini. Bring to a boil. Cook, partially covered, for 4 to 5 minutes until tender but firm.

Sprinkle Parmesan cheese over individual servings. Makes 9 cups (2.25 L).

1 cup (250 mL): 144 Calories; 2 g Total Fat (0.5 g Sat., 1 mg Cholesterol); 913 mg Sodium; 10 g Protein; 22 g Carbohydrate; 1 g Dietary Fiber

Pictured on page 126.

Note: If using commercial tortellini, add to soup at the same time as broccoli and green onion. Cook for 10 to 12 minutes until tortellini is tender but firm.

Spaetzle Soup

Spaetzle (SHPEHT-sehl) is German for "little sparrow." Spaetzle are tiny noodles.

Water	8 cups	2 L
Chicken (or vegetable) bouillon powder	¼ cup	60 mL
Sliced celery	1 cup	250 mL
Chopped celery leaves, packed	¼ cup	60 mL
Finely chopped onion	¼ cup	60 mL
Medium carrots, diced	2	2
Parsley flakes	1 tbsp.	15 mL
Bay leaf	1	1
All-purpose flour	1¼ cups	300 mL
Salt, sprinkle		
Frozen egg product, thawed	8 oz.	227 mL
Cold water, approximately	5 tbsp.	75 mL
Freshly ground pepper, sprinkle		

Combine first 8 ingredients in large saucepan or Dutch oven. Simmer, partially covered, for 30 minutes until onion is soft.

Combine flour, salt, egg product and 3 tbsp. (50 mL) water in small bowl. Mix until smooth. Stir in about 2 tbsp. (30 mL) water to make a sticky, paste-like mixture. To make spaetzle, squeeze dough through spaetzle maker, or push dough through holes of colander with back of spoon into simmering broth. Holes must be at least ³⁄₁₆ inch (4 mm) in diameter for the dough to go through. Cook for 3 to 5 minutes until tender but firm. Discard bay leaf.

Sprinkle with pepper. Makes about 12 cups (3 L).

1 cup (250 mL): 79 Calories; 0.8 g Total Fat (0.2 g Sat., 0.5 mg Cholesterol); 704 mg Sodium; 4 g Protein; 14 g Carbohydrate; 1 g Dietary Fiber

Italian Minestrone

Rich red broth with lots of vegetables and pasta. Very satisfying.
Takes only 15 minutes to chop vegetables.

Chopped onion	1 cup	250 mL
Garlic cloves, minced	2	2
Olive oil	2 tsp.	10 mL
Chopped celery, with some leaves	1 cup	250 mL
Water	8 cups	2 L
Canned tomatoes, with juice, chopped or lightly processed	28 oz.	796 mL
Vegetable bouillon powder	1 tbsp.	15 mL
Parsley flakes	1 tbsp.	15 mL
Dried thyme, crushed	1 tsp.	5 mL
Chili powder	1/2 tsp.	2 mL
Salt	1/2 tsp.	2 mL
Ground rosemary	1/8 tsp.	0.5 mL
Bay leaf	1	1
Cayenne pepper, pinch		
Diced carrot	2 cups	500 mL
Diced zucchini, with peel	1 1/2 cups	375 mL
Finely chopped cabbage	1 cup	250 mL
Canned red kidney beans, with liquid	2 x 14 oz.	2 x 398 mL
Canned white beans, drained	14 oz.	398 mL
Elbow macaroni (small pasta), 4 oz. (113 g)	1 cup	250 mL
Boiling water	6 cups	1.5 L
Salt	1 1/2 tsp.	7 mL
Grated fresh Parmesan cheese, sprinkle (optional)		

Sauté onion and garlic in oil in Dutch oven for 1 minute. Add celery. Sauté for 3 to 4 minutes until onion is soft.

Add next 13 ingredients. Bring mixture to a boil. Simmer, partially covered, for 40 minutes until carrot is tender.

Fork mash about 1/2 can of kidney beans. Stir into soup. Add remaining kidney beans and white beans. Simmer, partially covered, for 20 minutes.

Cook macaroni in boiling water and second amount of salt in large saucepan for 7 to 8 minutes, stirring occasionally, until tender but firm. Drain well. Add to soup. Sprinkle individual servings with Parmesan cheese. Makes 17 cups (4.25 L), enough to feed a crowd!

1 cup (250 mL): 115 Calories; 1.2 g Total Fat (0.2 g Sat., 0.1 mg Cholesterol); 484 mg Sodium; 6 g Protein; 21 g Carbohydrate; 5 g Dietary Fiber

Pictured on page 126.

Asparagus Leek Soup

To save time, start chopping vegetables for the broth while chicken is poaching.

Boneless, skinless chicken breast half	¼ lb.	113 g
White (or alcohol-free white) wine	¼ cup	60 mL
Condensed chicken broth	3 × 10 oz.	3 × 284 mL
Water	4 cups	1 L
Medium leek (white and tender green parts only), see Tip, below	1	1
Finely diced red or yellow pepper	½ cup	125 mL
Fresh asparagus, sliced into 1 inch (2.5 cm) lengths	1 lb.	454 g
Uncooked fusilli (spiral pasta), 3½ oz. (100 g)	1 cup	250 mL
Finely chopped fresh parsley (or 2 tsp., 10 mL, dried)	2 tbsp.	30 mL
Pepper	⅛ tsp.	0.5 mL

Place chicken breast and wine in small non-stick skillet. Cook, covered, for 3 to 4 minutes on each side. Remove lid. Cook until liquid is evaporated and chicken is well browned on both sides. Remove chicken to cutting board. Cut into slivers.

Combine chicken broth and water in Dutch oven. Ladle a bit of broth into skillet used to cook chicken. Pour all brown flavoring back into broth in Dutch oven. This adds great flavor to the soup.

Thinly slice leek crosswise. Add to broth. Add red pepper. Bring mixture to a boil. Simmer, partially covered, for 20 minutes.

Add asparagus, pasta and chicken. Cook for 12 to 15 minutes, partially covered, until asparagus and pasta are tender.

Stir in parsley and pepper. Makes 9 cups (2.25 L).

1 cup (250 mL): 108 Calories; 1.5 g Total Fat (0.4 g Sat., 8.3 mg Cholesterol); 642 mg Sodium; 10 g Protein; 12 g Carbohydrate; 2 g Dietary Fiber

Pictured on page 125.

 To wash leeks thoroughly, cut in half lengthwise. Hold cut sides under cold running water to remove dirt.

Pierogies

A Polish specialty. Serve with Mushroom Dill Sauce, page 110, or light sour cream.

PIEROGI DOUGH		
Prepared Basic Pasta Dough, page 86	1½ lbs.	680 g
POTATO AND CHEESE FILLING		
Baking potatoes, peeled	1 lb.	454 g
Boiling water	2 cups	500 mL
Grated light Cheddar cheese	½ cup	125 mL
Onion powder	¼ tsp.	1 mL
Salt	½ tsp.	2 mL
Pepper	⅛ tsp.	0.5 mL
SAUERKRAUT FILLING		
Finely chopped onion	2 tbsp.	30 mL
Tub margarine	1 tsp.	5 mL
Sauerkraut, well drained and chopped	2 cups	500 mL
Mashed potato	⅓ cup	75 mL
Pepper	⅛ tsp.	0.5 mL
Boiling water	3 qts.	3 L
Salt	1 tbsp.	15 mL

Pierogi Dough: Roll out ⅓ of rested dough very thinly (about ¹/₁₆ inch, 1.5 mm) on lightly floured surface.

1. Cut out circles, using 3 inch (7.5 cm) cookie cutter. Spoon 2 tsp. (10 mL) of your choice of filling onto center of each circle of dough.

2. Fold in half and press wet edges together to seal. Place on ungreased baking sheet. Cover with tea towel. Keep pierogies covered as you work to prevent them from drying out. At this point pierogies may be frozen on baking sheet and then removed to a freezer bag.

Gently drop about 15 pierogies at a time into boiling water and salt in Dutch oven. Return to a boil. Cook for about 3 minutes, stirring often, until all pierogies look puffed and float to surface. If cooking from frozen state, cook for 5 to 6 minutes. Remove with slotted spoon. Rinse with warm water. Drain. Eat immediately or drizzle warm chicken broth over top. Cover and keep warm in low oven. Makes 48 pierogies.

(continued on next page)

Potato And Cheese Filling: Cook potatoes in boiling water in medium saucepan for about 25 minutes until tender. Drain, reserving about ½ cup (125 mL) cooking water. Mash potatoes very well, adding cheese, onion powder, salt and pepper. Add a bit of reserved water, as needed, to moisten potato. Makes 2 cups (500 mL) filling.

Sauerkraut Filling: Sauté onion in margarine in medium non-stick skillet until soft. Add sauerkraut. Sauté until slightly dry. Add mashed potato and pepper. Mix well. Cool before filling. Makes 2 cups (500 mL) filling.

1 pierogi with Potato And Cheese Filling: 41 Calories; 0.3 g Total Fat (0.2 g Sat., 0.8 mg Cholesterol); 93 mg Sodium; 1 g Protein; 8 g Carbohydrate; trace Dietary Fiber

1 pierogi with Sauerkraut Filling: 34 Calories; 0.2 g Total Fat (trace Sat., 0 mg Cholesterol); 106 mg Sodium; 1 g Protein; 7 g Carbohydrate; 1 g Dietary Fiber

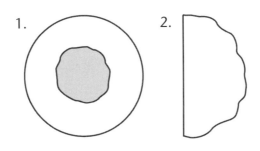

Paré Pointer

Throw your laundry in the ocean and it will be washed ashore.

Spinach And Cheese Cappelletti

Cute little "hats" stuffed with a green and white filling.

FILLING

Garlic clove, minced (optional)	1	1
Finely chopped onion	2 tbsp.	30 mL
Tub margarine	1 tsp.	5 mL
Frozen spinach, thawed, squeezed dry and finely chopped	1/3 x 10 oz.	1/3 x 300 g
Dry curd cottage cheese	1/2 cup	125 mL
Egg white (large)	1	1
Non-fat cream cheese	2 tbsp.	30 mL
Grated light Parmesan cheese product	1 tbsp.	15 mL
Salt	3/4 tsp.	4 mL
Parsley flakes	1/4 tsp.	1 mL
Dried marjoram, crushed	1/4 tsp.	1 mL
Dried sweet basil, crushed	1/4 tsp.	1 mL
Freshly ground pepper, sprinkle		
Prepared Egg Pasta Dough, page 87 (or Basic Pasta Dough, page 86), about 1/3 of recipe (see Note)	1/2 lb.	225 g
Boiling water	3 qts.	3 L
Salt	1 tbsp.	15 mL

Filling: Sauté garlic and onion in margarine until onion is soft. Stir in spinach. Cook for 30 seconds to dry.

Put next 9 ingredients into blender. Add spinach mixture. Process, with an on/off motion, until spinach is well chopped and cheeses are evenly moistened. Makes 3/4 cup (175 mL) filling.

1. Roll out 1/4 of rested dough into very thin 12 x 16 inch (30 x 40 cm) rectangle. Cut 2 inch (5 cm) wide strips. Place slightly rounded 1/4 tsp. (1 mL) filling, about 1 1/2 inches (3.8 cm) apart, on dough starting 3/4 inch (2 cm) from one edge. Cut dough between dabs of filling with sharp knife to form squares.

2. Moisten 2 adjacent sides of each square with water. Fold moistened edge diagonally over filling.

3. a) Seal edges making small filled triangle.

   b) Bend each triangle around finger, at fold, and pinch 2 ends together, making sure the pointy corner is up to resemble tiny hat. Repeat until all dough and filling are used. Keep pasta in single layer on floured tray, covered with tea towel until ready to cook.

(continued on next page)

Stuffed Pastas

Cook cappelletti in 2 batches in gently boiling water and second amount of salt in Dutch oven for 2 to 3 minutes (note that these take less time to cook than mushroom tortellini, because they are smaller in size), stirring occasionally, until tender but firm. Remove with slotted spoon to colander. Rinse with hot water. Drain. Makes about 130, enough for 8 servings.

1 serving: 90 Calories; 0.9 g Total Fat (0.2 g Sat., 1 mg Cholesterol); 424 mg Sodium; 6 g Protein; 14 g Carbohydrate; 1 g Dietary Fiber

Pictured on page 144.

Note: Using durum semolina instead of flour in the dough makes a roll that is firmer and easier to handle.

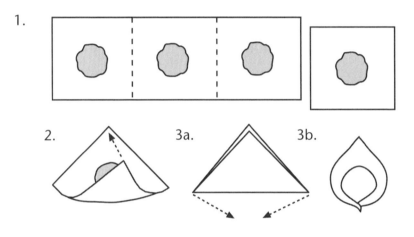

Jumbo Cheese Shells

You can find jumbo shell pasta at Italian specialty stores.

All-purpose flour	4 tsp.	20 mL
Skim evaporated milk	¾ cup	175 mL
Finely chopped onion	½ cup	125 mL
Garlic clove, minced	1	1
Olive oil	1 tsp.	5 mL
Canned plum tomatoes, processed	14 oz.	398 mL
Finely chopped fresh sweet basil	¼ cup	60 mL
(or 1 tbsp., 15 mL, dried)		
Salt	¼ tsp.	1 mL
Jumbo shell pasta (8 oz., 225 g)	24	24
Boiling water	3 qts.	3 L
Salt	1 tbsp.	15 mL
Part-skim ricotta cheese	1 cup	250 mL
Non-fat creamed cottage cheese,	1 cup	250 mL
sieved or mashed		
Egg whites (large), fork-beaten	2	2
Grated light Parmesan cheese product	1 tbsp.	15 mL
Salt, sprinkle		
Pepper	¹⁄₁₆ tsp.	0.5 mL

Measure flour into small saucepan. Slowly whisk in evaporated milk over medium until boiling and thickened. Remove from heat. Cover.

Sauté onion and garlic in oil in medium non-stick skillet until soft. Stir in tomato, basil and first amount of salt. Cover. Simmer for 10 minutes. Stir in milk mixture. Simmer, stirring constantly, until boiling and thickened. Pour into ungreased 9 x 13 inch (22 x 33 cm) baking dish.

Cook pasta shells in boiling water and second amount of salt in large saucepan for 10 to 12 minutes, stirring carefully to prevent shells from ripping. Pasta should be slightly undercooked. Drain and rinse well with cold water. Turn upside down on a clean dry cloth to drain well.

Combine remaining 6 ingredients in small bowl. Mix well. Fill each shell with rounded tablespoonful of cheese mixture. Arrange shells over tomato sauce. Cover with foil. Bake in 350°F (175°C) oven for 50 minutes. Drizzle sauce from baking dish over pasta to serve. Makes 2 cups (500 mL) sauce and 24 shells. Serves 4.

1 serving: 457 Calories; 7.9 g Total Fat (3.7 g Sat., 22.5 mg Cholesterol); 645 mg Sodium; 34 g Protein; 63 g Carbohydrate; 3 g Dietary Fiber

Pictured on page 143.

Swiss Rolled Pasta

Very attractive presentation. Can be made ahead
and reheated (see Tip, page 147).

Prepared Egg Pasta Dough, page 87, (½ of recipe)	¾ lb.	340 g
Frozen chopped spinach, thawed	2 × 10 oz.	2 × 300 g
Salt	½ tsp.	2 mL
Lemon pepper	¼ tsp.	1 mL
Chopped non-fat ham	2 × 4 oz.	2 × 125 g
Green onions, sliced	3	3
Grated Romano cheese	2 tbsp.	30 mL
Boiling water, to cover		
Salt	1 tbsp.	15 mL
SWISS CHEESE SAUCE		
Skim evaporated milk	13½ oz.	385 mL
All-purpose flour	3 tbsp.	50 mL
Non-fat spreadable cream cheese	¼ cup	60 mL
Grated light Swiss cheese	½ cup	125 mL
Ground nutmeg, pinch		
Pepper	⅛ tsp.	0.5 mL
Chopped fresh parsley	1 tbsp.	15 mL

Roll out rested dough to 10 × 12 inch (25 × 30 cm) rectangle.

Squeeze out any excess water from spinach. Chop well. Sprinkle over pasta sheet, spreading and packing down lightly in even layer to within 1 inch (2.5 cm) of edges. Sprinkle with first amount of salt and lemon pepper. Cover with ham, green onion and Romano cheese. Roll firmly but gently from long side, like jelly roll. Moisten long edge of pasta to seal lightly. Place roll, seam side down, on 4 layers of cheesecloth or tea towel. Wrap roll in cheesecloth firmly, tying ends closed (like a Christmas "cracker" with butcher's string).

Bring water and second amount of salt to boil in large roaster fitted with wire rack. Gently lower roll into water and add enough additional boiling water to cover. Simmer gently, covered, for 30 minutes. Carefully remove from water with 2 slotted spoons or lifters to support both ends so roll doesn't split in middle. Place on serving tray. Remove cheesecloth gently. Cool slightly before cutting.

Swiss Cheese Sauce: Combine evaporated milk and flour until smooth. Heat, stirring frequently, until boiling and thickened. Remove from heat. Add remaining 5 ingredients, stirring until cheese is melted. Makes 1⅔ cups (400 mL) sauce. Slice warm roll and arrange on platter. Serve immediately with hot cheese sauce drizzled over top. Cuts into 12 slices.

1 slice: 153 Calories; 1.7 g Total Fat (0.8 g Sat., 5.5 mg Cholesterol); 622 mg Sodium; 12 g Protein; 23 g Carbohydrate; 2 g Dietary Fiber

Pictured on page 143.

Leek And Spinach Manicotti

Bright green filling. Lots of sauce. To fill manicotti shells, try using a plastic freezer bag with 1 corner cut off, or a pastry bag with a large tip.

Finely sliced leek (white and tender green parts only), see Tip, page 131	3 cups	750 mL
Garlic cloves, minced	2	2
Olive oil	2 tsp.	10 mL
Water	1 tbsp.	15 mL
Fresh spinach, well packed, coarsely chopped	6 cups	1.5 L
Herb-flavored non-fat spreadable cream cheese	1/4 cup	60 mL
Dry curd cottage cheese	1 1/2 cups	375 mL
Egg whites (large)	2	2
Salt	1/2 tsp.	2 mL
Dried sweet basil	1/2 tsp.	2 mL
Dried whole oregano	1/4 tsp.	1 mL
Ground nutmeg, pinch		
Manicotti shells	14	14
Boiling water	3 qts.	3 L
Salt	1 tbsp.	15 mL
Finely chopped onion	1/4 cup	60 mL
Olive oil	1 tsp.	5 mL
Canned tomatoes, processed	28 oz.	796 mL
Salt	1/2 tsp.	2 mL
Granulated sugar, pinch		
Grated part-skim mozzarella cheese	1/2 cup	125 mL

Sauté leek and garlic in first amount of oil and water in large non-stick skillet for about 15 minutes until leek is tender. Stir in spinach. Cover. Cook for 5 minutes until spinach is wilted. Remove cover. Cook for about 1 minute until liquid is evaporated. Stir in cream cheese until melted.

Mix cottage cheese and egg whites in small bowl until quite smooth. Stir into spinach mixture. Add first amount of salt, basil, oregano and nutmeg. Stir well.

Cook manicotti shells in 2 batches in boiling water and second amount of salt in Dutch oven for 7 minutes, stirring occasionally. Pasta should still be quite firm. Drain and rinse in cold water. Drain well.

Spoon 1/4 cup (60 mL) filling into each manicotti. Place manicotti in single layer in lightly greased 9 x 13 inch (22 x 33 cm) baking dish.

Sauté onion in second amount of oil in large non-stick skillet, stirring frequently, until soft. Add tomato, third amount of salt and sugar. Boil rapidly, uncovered, for 1 minute. Pour sauce over manicotti. Sprinkle with cheese. Cover tightly with lightly greased foil. Bake in 350°F (175°C) oven for 30 minutes until hot and bubbling. Makes 14 manicotti.

1 filled manicotti with sauce: 132 Calories; 2.3 g Total Fat (0.7 g Sat., 3.6 mg Cholesterol); 340 mg Sodium; 8 g Protein; 20 g Carbohydrate; 2 g Dietary Fiber

Pictured on page 54.

 Stuffed Pastas

Spinach-Stuffed Cannelloni

Assemble everything the day before or morning of. Cover and refrigerate.
Bake when needed. To fill cannelloni shells, try using a plastic freezer bag with
1 corner cut off, or a pastry bag with a large tip.

TOMATO SAUCE

Canned stewed tomatoes, mashed or processed	28 oz.	796 mL
Water	1 cup	250 mL
Brown sugar, packed	1 tsp.	5 mL
Whole cloves	2	2
Garlic clove, minced	1	1
Dried whole oregano	1/2 tsp.	2 mL

SPINACH FILLING

Finely chopped onion	1/3 cup	75 mL
Olive oil	1 tsp.	5 mL
Frozen chopped spinach, thawed and squeezed dry	10 oz.	300 g
Non-fat spreadable cream cheese	1/2 cup	125 mL
Non-fat creamed cottage cheese, mashed	1 cup	250 mL
Egg whites (large), fork-beaten	2	2
Grated light Parmesan cheese product	1 tbsp.	15 mL
Salt	1/2 tsp.	2 mL
Pepper	1/8 tsp.	0.5 mL
Ground nutmeg	1/8 tsp.	0.5 mL
Oven-ready cannelloni shells	15	15
Grated part-skim mozzarella cheese	1/2 cup	125 mL

Tomato Sauce: Combine all 6 ingredients in medium saucepan. Cover. Cook for 30 minutes. Discard cloves. Pour 1/2 of sauce into ungreased 2 quart (2 L) shallow casserole dish or 9 x 13 inch (22 x 33 cm) baking dish. Reserve remaining 1/2 of sauce.

Spinach Filling: Sauté onion in oil in large non-stick skillet until soft. Add spinach. Stir until liquid is evaporated. Remove from heat. Add cream cheese. Stir until cheese is melted.

Add cottage cheese, egg whites, Parmesan cheese, salt, pepper and nutmeg. Stir.

Divide and spoon filling into each cannelloni. Arrange in single layer over tomato sauce in casserole dish. Drizzle with remaining sauce, making sure there is some on every tube. Cover with lightly greased foil. Bake in 350°F (175°C) oven for 40 minutes until pasta is tender and liquid is almost evaporated. Remove foil. Sprinkle with mozzarella cheese. Bake, uncovered, for 5 to 10 minutes until cheese is melted. Makes 15 cannelloni.

1 cannelloni with sauce: 93 Calories; 1.4 g Total Fat (0.6 g Sat., 2.5 mg Cholesterol); 257 mg Sodium; 7 g Protein; 13 g Carbohydrate; 2 g Dietary Fiber

Pictured on page 72 and back cover.

Cannelloni St. Jacques

A very attractive dish with plenty of sauce. A nice recipe to serve to company.

Water	1 cup	250 mL
White (or alcohol-free white) wine	1/4 cup	60 mL
Bay leaf	1	1
Fresh sprigs parsley	2	2
Seafood bouillon powder	2 tsp.	10 mL
Small fresh (or frozen, thawed) scallops	3/4 lb.	340 g
All-purpose flour	1/4 cup	60 mL
Skim evaporated milk	1 cup	250 mL
Salt	1/4 tsp.	1 mL
Freshly ground pepper, sprinkle		
Prepared Egg Pasta Dough, page 87 (1/2 of recipe)	12 oz.	340 g
Water, divided	4 tbsp.	60 mL
Skim evaporated (or skim) milk	1 tbsp.	15 mL
Grated light Parmesan cheese product	2 tbsp.	30 mL
Grated part-skim mozzarella cheese	1/4 cup	60 mL
Roasted red pepper or pimiento strips, for garnish		

Combine first 5 ingredients in medium saucepan. Bring to a boil. Add scallops. When mixture returns to a boil, time for about 2 minutes, until scallops are just cooked. Remove scallops with slotted spoon to small bowl, leaving cooking liquid in saucepan.

Combine flour and first amount of evaportated milk in small bowl until smooth. Whisk into cooking liquid. Cook, stirring frequently, until mixture is thickened. Season with salt and pepper. Reserve 1 cup (250 mL) of sauce for topping. Stir scallops into remaining sauce.

Divide rested pasta dough in half. Roll out each half out on lightly floured surface to about 11 x 11 inch (28 x 28 cm) square. Trim edges with ruler and sharp knife to 10 x 10 inches (25 x 25 cm). (Save pasta scraps for Leek And Potato Soup, page 128.) Cut through center lengthwise and crosswise to make four 5 x 5 inch (12.5 x 12.5 cm) squares. Place about 1/4 cup (60 mL) filling in center of each square. Moisten one edge with small paintbrush, or your fingertip, dipped in water. Bring 2 opposite sides together around filling, overlapping edges to seal lightly.

(continued on next page)

Pour 2 tbsp. (30 mL) water in bottom of lightly greased 3 quart (3 L) shallow casserole dish or 9 × 13 inch (22 × 33 cm) baking dish. Lay filled cannelloni, seam side down, in single layer in bottom of casserole dish. Pour remaining 2 tbsp. (30 mL) water over each cannelloni. Cover tightly with lid or foil. Bake in 350°F (175°C) oven for 15 minutes.

Stir second amount of evaporated milk into reserved sauce. Thin slightly to make barely pourable consistency. Stir in Parmesan cheese. Pour over each cannelloni to cover completely. Sprinkle with mozzarella cheese. Arrange red pepper strips over each cannelloni. Bake, uncovered, in 350°F (175°C) oven for about 25 minutes until hot and bubbling and surface is golden. Makes 8 stuffed cannelloni.

1 stuffed cannelloni: 200 Calories; 1.7 g Total Fat (0.7 g Sat., 18.3 mg Cholesterol); 587 mg Sodium; 16 g Protein; 28 g Carbohydrate; 1 g Dietary Fiber

Pictured on page 53.

 When making stuffed pasta, it is important to keep the dough from drying out. To avoid this, keep the dough you aren't working with wrapped tightly in plastic wrap.

Paré Pointer
She thought she could knit a barbed wire fence with steel wool.

Shrimp And Meat Wontons

These have a pretty fluted edge. Wontons can be individually frozen,
uncooked, on a large baking sheet and then transferred to a freezer bag.
Cook in boiling soup or broth from the frozen state for 6 to 7 minutes.

Cooked shrimp, chopped	1/4 lb.	113 g
Lean ground chicken (or pork)	1/4 lb.	113 g
Egg white (large)	1	1
Hoisin (or black bean) sauce	2 tsp.	10 mL
Cornstarch	2 tsp.	10 mL
Garlic powder	1/2 tsp.	2 mL
Pepper, sprinkle		
Commercial wonton wrappers	55-60	55-60

Combine first 7 ingredients in small bowl. Mix well.

Place rounded 1/2 tsp. (2 mL) filling slightly off center on wrapper. Moisten finger in water and "draw" circle around filling. Fold wrapper in half over filling. Press and flute rounded edge to seal. Repeat with remaining filling and wrappers. Cover wontons with damp tea towel to keep from drying out until ready to cook.

Boil in Wonton Soup, page 127, or broth, for about 4 minutes until meat is cooked and wrappers are tender. Makes 55 to 60 wontons, enough for 10 servings.

1 serving: *62 Calories; 0.6 g Total Fat (0.1 g Sat., 30.8 mg Cholesterol); 153 mg Sodium; 6 g Protein; 8 g Carbohydrate; trace Dietary Fiber*

1. Jumbo Cheese Shells, page 136
2. Cold Garlic Cream Sauce, page 114
3. Curried Shrimp Roll, page 146
4. Swiss Rolled Pasta with Swiss Cheese Sauce, page 137
5. Easy Spicy Tomato Sauce, page 110

Props Courtesy Of: Eaton's

Crunchy Vegetarian Wontons

Wontons can be individually frozen, uncooked, on large baking sheet and then transferred to freezer bag. Cook in boiling soup or broth from frozen state for 6 to 7 minutes.

Canned water chestnuts, drained, finely chopped and blotted dry	$\frac{1}{2}$ cup	125 mL
Finely chopped bean sprouts	$\frac{1}{2}$ cup	125 mL
Finely chopped Chinese cabbage	$\frac{1}{2}$ cup	125 mL
Green onion, finely chopped	1	1
Egg white (large)	1	1
Hoisin (or black bean) sauce	2 tsp.	10 mL
Cornstarch	1 tsp.	5 mL
Grated gingerroot	$\frac{1}{2}$ tsp.	2 mL
Salt	$\frac{1}{4}$ tsp.	1 mL
Garlic powder	$\frac{1}{8}$ tsp.	0.5 mL
Commercial wonton wrappers	55-60	55-60

Place first 10 ingredients in small bowl. Stir to combine. Transfer to strainer set in small bowl to allow accumulating liquid to drain while filling wontons.

Place rounded $\frac{1}{2}$ tsp. (2 mL) filling slightly off center on wrapper. Moisten finger in water and "draw" circle around filling. Fold wrapper in half over filling. Press and flute rounded edge to seal. Repeat with remaining filling and wrappers. Cover wontons with damp tea towel to keep from drying out until ready to cook.

Boil in Wonton Soup, page 127, or broth, for 4 minutes until wrappers are tender. Makes 55 to 60 wontons, enough for 10 servings.

1 serving: 47 Calories; 0.2 g Total Fat (trace Sat., 1.4 mg Cholesterol); 189 mg Sodium; 2 g Protein; 9 g Carbohydrate; trace Dietary Fiber

1. Roasted Pepper And Tomato Sauce, page 109
2. Spinach And Cheese Cappelletti, page 134
3. Zucchini And Mushroom Sauce, page 115
4. Bolognese Sauce, page 114
5. Sauced Chicken With Pasta Pancakes, page 32

Props Courtesy Of: The Bay

Curried Shrimp Roll

Serve with cold yogurt sauce (such as Tzatziki Dressing, page 94) drizzled over top or served on the side. Can be made ahead and reheated (see Tip, page 147).

All-purpose flour (see Note)	1¹/₂ cups	375 mL
Paprika	1 tbsp.	15 mL
Chili powder	1 tsp.	5 mL
Salt	¹/₂ tsp.	2 mL
Cayenne pepper	¹/₄ tsp.	1 mL
Warm water	¹/₂ cup	125 mL
Garlic cloves, minced	2	2
Chopped onion	²/₃ cup	150 mL
Large yellow pepper, seeded and chopped	1	1
Tub margarine	1 tsp.	5 mL
Curry paste (available in ethnic section of grocery stores)	2 tsp.	10 mL
Fresh shrimp, peeled and deveined (or 2 cups, 500 mL, cooked)	³/₄ lb.	340 g
Canned water chestnuts, drained and chopped	8 oz.	227 mL
Salt	¹/₂ tsp.	2 mL
Water	3 qts.	3 L
Salt	1 tbsp.	15 mL

Combine first 5 ingredients in bowl of food processor. Slowly add warm water, using more or less, through feed tube while processing until flour is moistened and dough forms ball. Turn out onto lightly floured surface. Knead until smooth. Cover with plastic wrap. Let rest for 15 minutes.

Saute garlic, onion and yellow pepper in margarine in large non-stick skillet for 5 to 6 minutes, stirring frequently, until vegetables are very soft.

Stir in curry paste and shrimp. Stir together for 4 to 5 minutes until shrimp is cooked. (If using cooked shrimp, only stir together for 2 to 3 minutes.) Stir in water chestnuts and second amount of salt. Cool.

Roll out dough to 10 × 12 inch (25 × 30 cm) rectangle. Spread shrimp mixture in even layer over pasta sheet to within 1 inch (2.5 cm) of edges. Roll firmly but gently from long side, like jelly roll. Moisten long edge of pasta to seal lightly. Place roll, seam side down, on 4 layers of cheesecloth or on tea towel. Enclose roll in cheesecloth by wrapping firmly and tying ends closed (like a Christmas "cracker") with butcher's string.

(continued on next page)

Stuffed Pastas

Bring water and third amount of salt to a boil in large roaster fitted with rack. Gently lower roll into water and add enough additional boiling water to cover. Simmer gently, covered, for 30 minutes. Carefully remove from boiling water with 2 slotted spoons or lifters to support both ends so roll doesn't split in middle. Place on serving tray. Remove cheesecloth gently. Cool slightly before trimming ends and cutting. Serve immediately. Cuts into 12 slices.

1 slice: *112 Calories; 1.2 g Total Fat (0.2 g Sat., 43.1 mg Cholesterol); 277 mg Sodium; 8 g Protein; 17 g Carbohydrate; 1 g Dietary Fiber*

Pictured on page 143.

Note: Using durum semolina instead of flour in the dough makes a roll that is firmer and easier to handle.

To save time, Curried Shrimp Roll, page 146, and Swiss Rolled Pasta, page 137, can be made ahead. After slicing, rewrap and chill or freeze. On serving day, thaw slices and lay, slightly overlapping, in greased shallow casserole dish. Cover Curried Shrimp Roll slices with ¼ cup (60 mL) water; cover Swiss Rolled Pasta slices with Swiss Cheese Sauce, page 137. Bake, covered, in 350°F (175°C) oven for about 30 minutes until hot and bubbly.

Paré Pointer

He won't lend a dollar. He doesn't believe in passing the buck.

Mushroom-Filled Tortellini With Herb Butter

This dish is so good, you'll never believe it's low in fat! Make Herb Butter in the summer when fresh herbs are plentiful. Freeze in small amounts to enjoy all year.

MUSHROOM FILLING		
Garlic clove, minced	1	1
Finely chopped onion	½ cup	125 mL
Tub margarine	2 tsp.	10 mL
Chopped fresh mushrooms	2 cups	500 mL
Non-fat plain (or herb) spreadable cream cheese	2 tbsp.	30 mL
Seasoning salt	1 tsp.	5 mL
Freshly ground pepper, sprinkle		
Parsley flakes	2 tsp.	10 mL
Dried thyme, crushed	¼ tsp.	1 mL
Egg whites (large)	2	2
Fine dry bread crumbs	⅓ cup	75 mL

TORTELLINI		
Prepared Egg Pasta Dough, page 87 (or Basic Pasta Dough, page 86)	1½ lbs.	680 g
Boiling water	3 qts.	3 L
Salt	1 tbsp.	15 mL

HERB BUTTER		
Olive oil	1 tsp.	5 mL
Diet tub margarine	3 tbsp.	50 mL
Small garlic clove, minced	1	1
Finely chopped fresh parsley, packed	¼ cup	60 mL
Finely chopped fresh sweet basil, packed	¼ cup	60 mL
Finely chopped fresh dill weed, packed	2 tbsp.	30 mL
Finely chopped fresh oregano, packed	2 tbsp.	30 mL
Salt	¼ tsp.	1 mL

Grated light Parmesan cheese product, sprinkle (optional)

Mushroom Filling: Sauté garlic and onion in margarine for 1 minute. Add mushrooms. Sauté until soft. Cool mixture slightly. Put mushroom mixture into blender. Add cream cheese, seasoning salt, pepper, parsley, thyme and egg whites. Process until smooth. Remove to medium bowl. Add bread crumbs. Mix well. Makes about 1¼ cups (300 mL) filling.

(continued on next page)

148 Stuffed Pastas

Tortellini:

1. Roll out ¼ of rested dough into very thin large circle. Cut about twenty-five 2¼ inch (11 cm) circles of dough.
2. On each circle, place a rounded ½ tsp. (2 mL) filling in center. Moisten half of circle with water.
3. Fold dough over filling to seal edges.
4. Bend the fold over finger and join the 2 ends together.

Repeat until all dough and filling are used. Place pasta on floured tray. Cover with damp tea towel until ready to cook. Makes about 100 tortellini.

Cook tortellini in 3 batches in boiling water and salt in Dutch oven for 4 to 5 minutes, stirring occasionally, until tender but firm. Remove with sieve or slotted spoon to colander. Rinse with hot water. Drain. Place in serving dish.

Herb Butter: Combine all 8 ingredients in small bowl. Let stand for 10 minutes to allow flavors to blend. Makes about ⅔ cup (150 mL) butter.

Add Herb Butter to tortellini. Toss lightly. Sprinkle with Parmesan cheese. Serves 8.

1 serving: 266 Calories; 4.6 g Total Fat (0.8 g Sat., trace Cholesterol); 765 mg Sodium; 11 g Protein; 45 g Carbohydrate; 2 g Dietary Fiber

Pictured on the front cover.

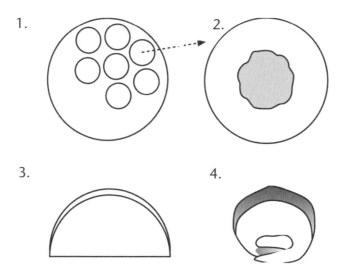

Mexican Chicken Rolls

Thick, creamy white sauce. So very rich, yet low in fat!

Skim evaporated milk	13½ oz.	385 mL
Skim milk	½ cup	125 mL
All-purpose flour	¼ cup	60 mL
Non-fat ranch dressing	½ cup	125 mL
Grated light Parmesan cheese product	¼ cup	60 mL
Grated light Monterey Jack cheese	1 cup	250 mL
Salsa	¼ cup	60 mL
Canned diced green chilies, well drained	4 oz.	114 mL
Diced cooked chicken (or turkey)	2½ cups	625 mL
Prepared Chili Pepper Pasta Dough, page 82	1¼ lbs.	560 g
Water, divided	4 tbsp.	60 mL
Grated light Cheddar cheese	½ cup	125 mL

Gradually whisk both milks into flour in large saucepan until smooth. Whisk in dressing. Cook over medium, stirring often, until boiling and thickened. Remove from heat. Stir in Parmesan cheese and Monterey Jack cheese until melted. Reserve 1½ cups (375 mL).

Stir salsa, green chilies and chicken into remaining sauce in saucepan.

Roll out ⅓ of rested pasta dough into 11 x 11 inch (28 x 28 cm) rectangle on lightly floured surface. Trim edges using ruler and sharp knife to make 10 x 10 inch (25 x 25 cm) rectangle. Cut straight line through center lengthwise and then crosswise to make four 5 x 5 inch (12.5 x 12.5 cm) squares. Spoon scant ⅓ cup (75 mL) filling in center of each square. Moisten 1 edge with water. Lift edges of dough over to form a roll and seal. Repeat until all dough and filling are used. Keep pasta covered with tea towel until ready to cook.

Pour 2 tbsp. (30 mL) water into lightly greased large shallow casserole dish or 9 x 13 inch (22 x 33 cm) baking dish. Lay rolls, seam side down, in single layer. Pour remaining 2 tbsp. (30 mL) water over rolls. Cover tightly with lid or lightly greased foil. Bake in 350°F (175°C) oven for 15 minutes. Pour reserved sauce over rolls. Sprinkle with Cheddar cheese. Cover. Bake in 350°F (175°C) oven for 15 minutes until cheese is melted. Makes 12 rolls.

1 roll: 246 Calories; 4.2 g Total Fat (2.1 g Sat., 36.5 mg Cholesterol); 688 mg Sodium; 22 g Protein; 29 g Carbohydrate; 1 g Dietary Fiber

Pictured on page 36.

Measurement Tables

Throughout this book measurements are given in Conventional and Metric measure. To compensate for differences between the two measurements due to rounding, a full metric measure is not always used. The cup used is the standard 8 fluid ounce. Temperature is given in degrees Fahrenheit and Celsius. Baking pan measurements are in inches and centimetres as well as quarts and litres. An exact metric conversion is given below as well as the working equivalent (Standard Measure).

Oven Temperatures

Fahrenheit (°F)	Celsius (°C)
175°	80°
200°	95°
225°	110°
250°	120°
275°	140°
300°	150°
325°	160°
350°	175°
375°	190°
400°	205°
425°	220°
450°	230°
475°	240°
500°	260°

Pans

Conventional Inches	Metric Centimetres
8x8 inch	20x20 cm
9x9 inch	22x22 cm
9x13 inch	22x33 cm
10x15 inch	25x38 cm
11x17 inch	28x43 cm
8x2 inch round	20x5 cm
9x2 inch round	22x5 cm
10x4^1/$_2$ inch tube	25x11 cm
8x4x3 inch loaf	20x10x7.5 cm
9x5x3 inch loaf	22x12.5x7.5 cm

Spoons

Conventional Measure	Metric Exact Conversion Millilitre (mL)	Metric Standard Measure Millilitre (mL)
1/8 teaspoon (tsp.)	0.6 mL	0.5 mL
1/4 teaspoon (tsp.)	1.2 mL	1 mL
1/2 teaspoon (tsp.)	2.4 mL	2 mL
1 teaspoon (tsp.)	4.7 mL	5 mL
2 teaspoons (tsp.)	9.4 mL	10 mL
1 tablespoon (tbsp.)	14.2 mL	15 mL

Cups

Conventional Measure	Metric Exact Conversion Millilitre (mL)	Metric Standard Measure Millilitre (mL)
1/4 cup (4 tbsp.)	56.8 mL	60 mL
1/3 cup (5^1/$_3$ tbsp.)	75.6 mL	75 mL
1/2 cup (8 tbsp.)	113.7 mL	125 mL
2/3 cup (10^2/$_3$ tbsp.)	151.2 mL	150 mL
3/4 cup (12 tbsp.)	170.5 mL	175 mL
1 cup (16 tbsp.)	227.3 mL	250 mL
4^1/$_2$ cups	1022.9 mL	1000 mL (1 L)

Dry Measurements

Conventional Measure Ounces (oz.)	Metric Exact Conversion Grams (g)	Metric Standard Measure Grams (g)
1 oz.	28.3 g	28 g
2 oz.	56.7 g	57 g
3 oz.	85.0 g	85 g
4 oz.	113.4 g	125 g
5 oz.	141.7 g	140 g
6 oz.	170.1 g	170 g
7 oz.	198.4 g	200 g
8 oz.	226.8 g	250 g
16 oz.	453.6 g	500 g
32 oz.	907.2 g	1000 g (1 kg)

Casseroles

CANADA & BRITAIN		UNITED STATES	
Standard Size Casserole	Exact Metric Measure	Standard Size Casserole	Exact Metric Measure
1 qt. (5 cups)	1.13 L	1 qt. (5 cups)	900 mL
1^1/$_2$ qts. (7^1/$_2$ cups)	1.69 L	1^1/$_2$ qts. (7^1/$_2$ cups)	1.35 L
2 qts. (10 cups)	2.25 L	2 qts. (10 cups)	1.8 L
2^1/$_2$ qts. (12^1/$_2$ cups)	2.81 L	2^1/$_2$ qts. (12^1/$_2$ cups)	2.25 L
3 qts. (15 cups)	3.38 L	3 qts. (15 cups)	2.7 L
4 qts. (20 cups)	4.5 L	4 qts. (20 cups)	3.6 L
5 qts. (25 cups)	5.63 L	5 qts. (25 cups)	4.5 L

Index

153

154

Photo Index

155

Tip Index

Brownies

*These are a very good substitute for high-fat brownies. They are moist and rich.
High in sugar so cut them small, and only indulge when you must have a sweet
chocolate treat.*

Frozen egg product, thawed	$^1/_2$ cup	125 mL
Canola oil	$^1/_4$ cup	60 mL
Jar of strained prunes (baby food)	4 $^1/_2$ oz.	128 mL
Vanilla	2 tsp.	10 mL
Brown sugar, packed	$^1/_2$ cup	125 mL
Granulated sugar	$^1/_2$ cup	125 mL
Cocoa	$^1/_2$ cup	125 mL
All-purpose flour	$^2/_3$ cup	150 mL
Baking powder	$^1/_2$ tsp.	2 mL
Salt	$^1/_8$ tsp.	0.5 mL
GLAZE (optional)		
Cocoa	1 tbsp.	15 mL
Icing (confectioner's) sugar	$^1/_2$ cup	125 mL
Hot water	1 tbsp.	15 mL

Beat egg product, canola oil, prunes and vanilla until smooth. Beat
in both sugars and cocoa. Beat in flour, baking powder and salt until
smooth. Pour into greased 8 x 8 inch (20 x 20 cm) baking pan. Bake
in 325°F (160°C) oven for 30 to 35 minutes just until center is set.
Do not overcook.

Glaze: Combine all 3 ingredients in small bowl until smooth. Drizzle over
warm brownies. Cool. Cuts into 25 squares.

NUTRITION INFORMATION 1 square: 78 Calories; 2.6 g Total Fat (0.3 g Sat., 0 mg Cholesterol);
26 mg Sodium; 1 g Protein; 14 g Carbohydrate; 1 g Dietary Fiber

CHOICES $^1/_2$ Fruit & Vegetable; 1 Sugar; $^1/_2$ Fat & Oil

Company's Coming cookbooks are available at **retail locations** throughout Canada!

See mail order form

Buy any 2 cookbooks—choose a 3rd FREE of equal or less value than the lowest price paid.   *Available in French

Original Series — CA$14.99 Canada — US$10.99 USA & International

CODE		CODE		CODE	
SQ	150 Delicious Squares*	FS	Fish & Seafood*	MU	Muffins & More*
AP	Appetizers	HE	Holiday Entertaining*	ODM	One-Dish Meals*
BA	Barbecues*	KC	Kids Cooking*	PA	Pasta*
BR	Breads*	LCA	Light Casseroles*	PI	Pies*
BB	Breakfasts & Brunches*	LR	Light Recipes*	PZ	Pizza!*
CK	Cakes	LFC	Low-Fat Cooking* NEW	PR	Preserves*
CA	Casseroles*	LFP	Low-Fat Pasta* NEW	SA	Salads*
CH	Chicken, Etc.*	LU	Lunches*	SC	Slow Cooker Recipes*
CO	Cookies*	MC	Main Courses	SS	Soups & Sandwiches
CT	Cooking For Two*	MAM	Make-Ahead Meals*	ST	Starters*
DE	Desserts	ME	Meatless Cooking*	SF	Stir-Fry*
DI	Dinners of the World	MI	Microwave Cooking*	PB	The Potato Book* NEW
				VE	Vegetables

Greatest Hits — CA$12.99 Canada — US$9.99 USA & International

CODE		CODE	
BML	Biscuits, Muffins & Loaves*	SAW	Sandwiches & Wraps*
DSD	Dips, Spreads & Dressings*	SAS	Soups & Salads*

Lifestyle Series — CA$16.99 Canada — US$12.99 USA & International

CODE		CODE		CODE	
GR	Grilling*	LFC	Low-fat Cooking*	LFP	Low-fat Pasta*

Special Occasion Series — CA$19.99 Canada — US$19.99 USA & International

CODE	
CE	Chocolate Everything* NEW
EE	Easy Entertaining* (hardcover)

Other — CA$19.99 Canada — US$15.99 USA & International

CODE	
BE	Beef Today! (softcover)

Company's Coming COOKBOOKS®

www.**companys**coming.com
visit our web-site

COMPANY'S COMING PUBLISHING LIMITED
2311 - 96 Street
Edmonton, Alberta, Canada T6N 1G3
Tel: (780) 450-6223 Fax: (780) 450-1857

Exclusive Mail Order Offer

See page 158 for list of cookbooks

Buy **2** Get **1** FREE!
Buy any 2 cookbooks—choose a **3rd FREE** of equal or less value than the lowest price paid.

Quantity	Code	Title	Price Each	Price Total
			$	$
		don't forget		
		to indicate your		
		free book(s).		
		(see exclusive mail order		
		offer above)		
		please print		
	TOTAL BOOKS (including FREE)	**TOTAL BOOKS PURCHASED:**	$	

	International		Canada & USA	
Plus Shipping & Handling (per destination)	$7.00	(one book)	$5.00	(1-3 books)
Additional Books (including FREE books)	$	($2.00 each)	$	($1.00 each)
Sub-Total	$		$	
Canadian residents add G.S.T(7%)			$	
TOTAL AMOUNT ENCLOSED	$		$	

The Fine Print

- Orders outside Canada must be **PAID IN US FUNDS** by cheque or money order drawn on Canadian or US bank or by credit card.
- Make cheque or money order payable to: **COMPANY'S COMING PUBLISHING LIMITED.**
- Prices are expressed in Canadian dollars for Canada, US dollars for USA & International and are subject to change without prior notice.
- Orders are shipped surface mail. For courier rates, visit our web-site: **www.companyscoming.com** or contact us: **Tel: (780) 450-6223 Fax: (780) 450-1857.**
- Sorry, no C.O.D.'s.

Gift Giving

- Let us help you with your gift giving!
- We will send cookbooks directly to the recipients of your choice if you give us their names and addresses.
- Please specify the titles you wish to send to each person.
- If you would like to include your personal note or card, we will be pleased to enclose it with your gift order.
- Company's Coming Cookbooks make excellent gifts: Birthdays, bridal showers, Mother's Day, Father's Day, graduation or any occasion...collect them all!

☐ MasterCard   ☐ VISA

Expiry date _____

Account # _____

Name of cardholder _____

Cardholder's signature _____

Shipping Address
Send the cookbooks listed above to:

Name: _____

Street: _____

City: _____   Prov./State: _____

Country: _____   Postal Code/Zip: _____

Tel: (   ) _____

E-mail address: _____

YES! Please send a catalogue: ☐ English ☐ French

Please mail or fax to:

Company's Coming Publishing Limited
2311 - 96 Street
Edmonton, Alberta, Canada   T6N 1G3
Fax: (780) 450-1857

Name:_____

Address:_____

_____

e-mail:_____

Reader Survey

**We welcome your comments and would love to hear from you.
Please take a few moments to give us your feedback.**

1. *Approximately what percentage of the cooking do you do in your home?*_____ %

2. *How many meals do you cook in your home in a typical week?*   _____

3. *How often do you refer to a cookbook (or other source) for recipes?*

❑ Everyday   ❑ 2 or 3 times a month   ❑ A few times a year
❑ A few times a week   ❑ Once a month   ❑ Never

4. *What recipe features are most important to you? Rank 1 to 7;
   (1 being most important, 7 being least important).*

—— Recipes for everyday cooking
—— Recipes for guests and entertaining
—— Easy recipes; quick to prepare, with everyday ingredients
—— Low-fat or health-conscious recipes
—— Recipes you can trust to work
—— Recipes using exotic ingredients
—— Recipes using fresh ingredients only

5. *What cookbook features are most important to you? Rank 1 to 6;
   (1 being most important, 6 being least important).*

—— Lots of color photographs of recipes
—— "How-to" instructions or photos
—— Helpful hints & cooking tips
—— Lay-flat binding (coil or plastic comb)
—— Well organized with complete index
—— Priced low

6. *How many cookbooks have you purchased in the last year?*

7. *Of these, how many were gifts?*_____   _____

8. *Age group*

❑ Under 18   ❑ 25 to 34   ❑ 45 to 54   ❑ 65+
❑ 18 to 24   ❑ 35 to 44   ❑ 55 to 64

9. *What do you like best about Company's Coming Cookbooks?*

_____

_____

10. *How could Company's Coming Cookbooks be improved?*

_____

_____

11. *Topics you would like to see published by Company's Coming:*

_____

_____

Thank you for sharing your views. We truly value your input.